OPPORTUNITIES

in

Film Careers

W9-CNA-075

OPPORTUNITIES

in

Film Careers

REVISED EDITION

JAN BONE AND ANA FERNANDEZ

VGM Career Books

Chicago New York San Francisco Lisbon London Madrid Mexico City
Milan New Delhi San Juan Seoul Singapore Sydney Toronto

3 3113 02332 0445

The *McGraw·Hill* Companies

Library of Congress Cataloging-in-Publication Data

Bone, Jan.
     Opportunities in film careers / Jan Bone and Ana Fernandez. — Rev. ed.
          p.   cm. (VGM opportunities series)
     ISBN 0-07-141163-1
     1. Motion pictures—Vocational guidance.   I. Fernandez, Ana.   II. Title.
III. Series.

     PN1995.9.P75B66   2004
     791.43'029373—dc22   2003025628

1 2 3 4 5 6 7 8 9 0   LBM/LBM   3 2 1 0 9 8 7 6 5 4

ISBN 0-07-141163-1

Interior design by Rattray Design

McGraw-Hill books are available at special quantity discounts to use as premiums and sales promotions, or for use in corporate training programs. For more information, please write to the Director of Special Sales, Professional Publishing, McGraw-Hill, Two Penn Plaza, New York, NY 10121-2298. Or contact your local bookstore.

This book is printed on acid-free paper.

CONTENTS

FOREWORD

I BELIEVE THAT the motion picture, no matter its country of origin, is the single most powerful communication force available today for a pleasant and peaceful world. Nations may quarrel about borders and economics; they may become surly about slights either real or imagined or incited by political policy, but the language of their films is universally understood in whatever countries they are shown. There is as yet no home media environment that can compare to the epic experience of seeing a film in a large-screened, stereo-sound-equipped theater, along with hundreds of other people who are experiencing it simultaneously.

Human nature is one of the few unalterable elements in a world continually shocked and tormented by changes. People will always want to get out of their homes to participate in shared social experiences in their communities. I don't believe that most families will ever prefer to be hostages in their living rooms, chained to their television sets, no matter how generous the quantity of the entertainment at their fingertips.

The great task is how to locate, nourish, and give heart to young creative talent, the one indispensable element in the future of this industry. To fill the screens of movie houses (and, yes, to fill all the channels in the home theater, too) will generate a need for people to think, write, produce, direct, and act in numbers and quality that I doubt exist today.

There is our great challenge—to find and develop the talent. What the public is interested in is what is on the screen, be that the screen of the television set or the screen in the theater. The public will support what creative talent produces, and the new technologies will fuel the demand for quantity. What the public increasingly will demand will be quality. I think there will also be an increasing demand in production for young persons of talent to make the movies and the television programs of the future.

Jack Valenti
President
Motion Picture Association of America, Inc.

PREFACE

EVERY WEEK MILLIONS of people go to the movies or watch movies at home on DVD or videotape. Most of them are not watching these movies alone, because inherently movies are not meant to be a solitary activity. Now, that's not to say that watching a movie or video alone is not a satisfying experience. It certainly is. But it is in an atmosphere of social gathering, be it a few close friends or a theater full of strangers from widely different socioeconomic, religious, educational, cultural, and philosophical backgrounds, that movies have their greatest impact.

Think about it. Almost from the start, making a movie or a video is a strongly collaborative effort. The germ of an idea, the initial concept may originate in one creative head, but from that point on, the process that involves taking that idea and turning it into a strip of film or videotape that can be viewed by others incorporates the input and work of many.

Movie making has a very short history. Unlike art or music, whose roots we can trace back thousands of years, in the case of art to prehistory, movies date back only to the late 1800s. It is amazing to consider the scientific discoveries and technological developments that have occurred since that time to make motion pictures, as we know them today, possible.

But a movie is not just a technological marvel; it is an art. Just like painters use canvas and paint, sculptors mold clay, and novelists put pencil to paper, movie making is an art form whose medium is film. Unlike these solitary artists, to create a film involves the creativity and contribution of many and diverse artists—all sharing a common vision and a common goal. The impact of the movie, however, like the impact of a book, a piece of music, a painting, will be different for each individual who views it.

It seems fitting to draw a comparison between the numerous and diverse professionals—artists, craftspeople, actors, technicians— needed to create a movie and the uncountable and equally diverse public for whom these movies provide enjoyment, entertainment, and reflection. It's an impressive collaboration no matter how you look at it.

Acknowledgments

THE AUTHOR AND reviser acknowledge with thanks the help given by the following persons and organizations:

Stanley Ackerman
Dominic Amator
Christine Walsh
   Angelos
Janette Boatwright
Chris Bone
Jeannie Bone
Marcia Borie
Tom Brinkmoeller
Scott Carlberg
Laura Carroll
Peter Cole
Chuck Collett
Ken Creekmore
Helen Davis

Lynette Duensing
Sandy Forman
Joseph Hlubucek
Tom and Mabeth Hope
Max Howard
Jim Jordan
Ken Jurek
Tichi Wilkerson Kassel
Ted Kaye
Claire Labine
George Malko
Anne McKay
Rod Merl
Ron Osgood
Steve Purcell

Linda Rheinstein
Cathy A. Savino
Elizabeth Stanley
Lara Stolman
Martin E. Waldman
David Werner
Mary Williamson
Diane Wynter
Donald Zimmerman
Academy of Canadian
Cinema and
Television
Academy of Motion
Picture Arts and
Sciences
American Film
Institute
The American Museum
of the Moving Image
Art Center College of
Design
Assistant Directors
Training Program
Association of
Canadian Film
Craftspeople
British Film Institute
Conference Express
Corporation for Public
Broadcasting

Directors Guild of
America, Inc.
Embassy of Australia
The Hollywood Reporter
Hope Reports
International Alliance
of Theatrical Stage
Employees
(I.A.T.S.E.)
International Television
Association (ITVA)
Koloa Public and
School Library staff
Metro Orlando Film
and Entertainment
Commission
Motion Picture
Association of
America
National Film Board of
Canada
National Film and
Television School
New York University
The Post Group
Sundance Institute
Telefilm Canada
University of
California, Los
Angeles (UCLA)

University of Southern
    California (USC)
Variety
Walt Disney Animation
Women in
    Communications, Inc.

Women in Film
Writers Guild of
    America, East
Writers Guild of
    America, West

1

Development of the Film Industry

You sit in a large dark room full of strangers, all facing the same direction. You watch the shaking face of an enraged man. He looks as though he will soon explode and the orchestral music tells you to expect something big. And then, it happens. The man walks around, becoming enormous and green. He's out of control. His foot bursts out of his shoe. His head crashes though a wall. He jumps through the roof. You have to see it to believe it.

No matter how many times we go to the movies, they can always amaze and fascinate us. It's been that way ever since people first began to study the moving image. But if Peter Mark Roget, author of the famous thesaurus, had not looked through a venetian blind, there might never have been a film production industry. In 1824 he addressed a paper on his observations that motion could be broken down into a series of separate phases to the Royal Society in London, inspiring the creation of "eye-deception" machines like the zoetrope, meant to create the illusion of animated drawings.

In 1839 a French painter named Daguerre developed a process for positive photography that we call daguerreotype, while an English scientist named William Henry Fox Talbot successfully demonstrated a negative photographic process that allowed for virtually unlimited positive prints to be produced from one negative.

Even as photography was still being invented, motion photography was being imagined and developed. But there could be no motion picture until the exposure time of an hour could be reduced. By 1870, in Philadelphia, Henry Renno Heyl was able to actually project a photographic motion picture on a screen. Seven years later, using a row of still cameras, Eadweard Muybridge, a British photographer working in California, recorded the motion phases of a running horse.

All these advances, however, were mere laboratory experiments. It took Thomas A. Edison's genius to understand that the fifty-foot-long, inch-wide sample of a new material called film (which George Eastman had developed in Rochester, New York) could be combined with Edison's newfangled machine to produce pictorial images.

In the United States, motion pictures became a phenomenon on April 14, 1894, when ten of Thomas Edison's peep-show kinetoscopes opened on Broadway in New York City. Reaction to the new devices was mixed. Crowds huddled together to see bits of prize fights and fragments of vaudeville acts, but shortly thereafter, a showing of *Dolorita in the Passion Dance* was suppressed by the Atlantic City, New Jersey, police.

The first cinematographic public showing took place at the Grand Café in Paris on December 28th, 1895, when the Lumiére brothers showed a terrified audience a moving photograph of a train headed toward them.

By 1903 the world's first story picture, *The Great Train Robbery*, was in production. When Pittsburgh showman John P. Harris began to charge a five-cent admission to his "nickelodeon," the idea spread, and so did motion pictures.

Longer movies, many from Europe, and the great silent screen stars ushered in a new era for film in the United States. In 1915 Charlie Chaplin signed a contract to make twelve two-reel comedies at the unheard-of sum of $670,000 for the series. The great movie boom was under way.

Growth of the Industry

With *The Birth of a Nation* (1915) and *Intolerance* (1916), D. W. Griffith revolutionized the movie into an art form that could include intimate as well as spectacularly epic moments within the same story. Both films had great success with audiences, and thus the feature film as we know it was born.

When the first talkie, *The Jazz Singer*, starring Al Jolson, was released in 1927, the art form and the industry were transformed again. The audience wanted sound. Artists and movie stars had to either adapt to the new technology or retire. Even Charlie Chaplin had to make the transition.

That same year, the Academy of Motion Picture Arts and Sciences was founded, with actor Douglas Fairbanks as its first president, to honor achievement and foster advancement in filmmaking. The first annual Academy Awards ceremony was held in 1929.

It was around this time that the town of Hollywood became the site for the building of movie studios. Already, industry notables were concerned with training future filmmakers. In 1929 two fencing partners—Douglas Fairbanks and Rufus B. von KleinSmid, president of the University of Southern California—decided to offer the first film course. Introduction to Photoplay, at the University of Southern California, was described as an effort to provide "such training in the science and art of moving pictures for its protégés as would service to raise the standards and ideals of the business to the plane of the highest and most dignified professions."

Members of the founding faculty included playwright and screenwriter Clara Beranger; director, playwright, and screenwriter William C. DeMille, brother of Cecil B.; Douglas Fairbanks; D. W. Griffith; Irving Thalberg; and Darryl Zanuck. The lectures they gave included instruction on writing for the screen, directing actors, using the camera as a storyteller, and producing. Modern aesthetics, art history, philosophy, and art direction also were included in the curriculum.

Movies became more popular than ever and the era of the movie moguls began. During the Depression, theaters attracted customers by offering premiums like sets of dishes. More importantly, they offered an escape, a getaway from the reality of breadlines and the WPA, the dust storms and mortgage foreclosures.

Life was simpler at the movies. Shirley Temple danced across American screens and into the hearts of millions. Mickey Rooney, as Andy Hardy, earnestly proclaimed the virtues of his mom's apple pie whenever he and Judy Garland weren't hatching backyard musicals.

Unions

Behind the screen during the Depression, however, all was not ideal in film production. The technicians and craftspeople who actually made the movies worked long hours for little pay. As a direct result of substantial pay cuts, the Screen Actors Guild was formed. The

Directors Guild of America, which also organized about this time, resolved to preserve creative freedom.

One of the most important craft unions in film production, the International Alliance of Theatrical Stage Employees and Moving Picture Machine Operators of the United States and Canada, best known as I.A.T.S.E. or the I.A., was expanding into Hollywood. The I.A.T.S.E. began in 1893, when show business was confined almost entirely to the stage. During the next twenty years, stage carpenters, property workers, and electricians pioneered a drive for union recognition in the theater. Finally they had established their craft as one of the highest paid and most respected in America.

Soon after the birth of the film industry, beginning in 1908, projectionists throughout North America were brought into I.A.T.S.E, winning a battle for union recognition and top wages. Later, in the twenties and thirties, union benefits were extended to the Hollywood studios and the vast network of film exchanges throughout the United States and Canada.

World War II and Beyond

During World War II, Hollywood began turning out training films to meet the needs of the armed services. Donald Duck started selling war bonds, and so did the stars. Those who could, enlisted. Those who couldn't, like Van Johnson (classified 4-F and ineligible because of an earlier motorcycle accident), found themselves teamed with a variety of female stars who needed leading men.

Postwar America saw the birth of a new form of home entertainment. In 1939 the opening of the New York World's Fair was broadcast on television. And on July 1, 1941, American commercial television began. When television was mostly live, it was still enough of a novelty that Tuesday became Uncle Miltie night, and movie admissions dropped precipitously. Former film star Lucille Ball found a whole new audience and a better-than-ever career with "I Love Lucy," and millions waited out with her the birth of "Little Ricky"—the first time a major television star had been photographed in an advanced state of real pregnancy.

According to one industry story, a gas station owner, tired of poor television reception in the Pennsylvania mountains, climbed the hill behind his station shortly after World War II. Reportedly he put up an antenna and ran a wire down the mountainside to his television set. That's how cable television was born.

In 1972, HBO became the first cable television network. A traditional broadcast-style microwave link was used to connect HBO from New York to a cable system in Wilkes-Barre, Pennsylvania. It continued to expand. Soon HBO decided to use satellite transmission to distribute all its programming. Other companies set up cable networks and jumped on board.

As technology developed, it became possible to record shows electronically on magnetic tape. Broadcasters began to switch to videotape production. By the eighties, the use of videotape had spread widely. But just as broadcast television had an impact on theatrical film production, a new distribution system changed what and where America watched.

In the early 1980s, the cable television industry experienced rapid growth, but it stalled in the latter part of the decade. In the 1990s, technology improved, allowing cable systems to send more than five hundred channels to a given home.

According to the U.S. Census Bureau, in 1990, 54.9 million American households had basic cable. By 2000, the number was up to 69.3 million, with 2.4 television sets in the average home.

Today viewers are as enamored of the moving image as ever. Technology continues to change what and how we watch. Computer-generated animation and special effects delight us in theaters. Video streaming on the Internet gives us increased and immediate access to anything and everything. Video-on-demand services (VOD) offer television consumers more control over what they watch and when.

For many years, high-definition television has been the talk of the industry. Now HDTV is a thing of the present, offering the highest resolution ever and an image of incredible clarity. This technology requires new cameras, new transmission equipment, and a new sensitivity to image quality on the part of professionals, but it gives broadcasters the chance to transmit three-dimensional images for the first time and even more motivation to keep the viewers viewing.

What does this mean for you? Sitting in a movie theater, watching the opening titles of a feature film, you've probably wondered more than once what it's really like to be "in the movies." Is it as fun as it looks? Could you succeed in such a business? This book doesn't have all the answers, but it can help you discover what a film career is like.

Film and Video

The difference between film and video can be summarized simply. Film is loaded in a camera. It can be used only once to obtain an image. After filming, it is developed in chemicals. Only then is it exposed to light and shown by means of a projector.

Videotape, on the other hand, combines electronic impulses of picture and sound on magnetic videotape that can be played back immediately after recording. Like audiotape, videotape is threaded on a recorder. It can be exposed to light. Because it is erasable it can be used again and again. Videotape is shown by means of a VCR on a television screen.

There are different formats of video. VHS is preferred for the private consumer because of its low cost. In the professional world, the preferred format has changed as technology has evolved. Digital video, which produces a higher quality image for a lower cost, is presently taking over as the format of choice in both realms. Private consumers can now create better movies cheaper with digital video, and it's easier to put them on DVDs than on videotapes.

Which is better, film or video? Each has advantages and disadvantages. Each is appropriate in different circumstances. However, the line between the two has blurred, since film editors no longer physically splice film. Instead they edit on computers.

For the purposes of this book, we will broadly define opportunities in film production as jobs in film and video, because you need to master both to compete in the current job market. You will learn about some of the personal qualities you need to succeed and where to get training and knowledge. Because unions and guilds are so important in feature film, we'll describe a few of them. We'll also give you job-hunting tips from the pros—those who have made it.

Professionals in the film industry work long, hard hours. Because of the high cost and complicated process, they are under intense pressure. But in general, those in film say their job is exciting and rewarding.

2

How Film Is Made

So, you have an idea for a movie. You think you'll borrow a mini-DV camera, recruit some friends to act, shoot the story line in your backyard, send the film to the Sundance Festival, and get it distributed. No problem. But you know it's not really that easy, right?

In the last decade, with the advance of digital video technology and desktop editing software, moviemaking has become a much more affordable and accessible art form than it was in the past. This makes it easier for you (and for everybody else) to make a film.

But if you want to make a real film, a film that can be distributed in theaters or aired on commercial television, there are many details to pay attention to and many skills to be used. It is still a complex and very expensive process. Even small independent productions usually require a lighting crew, makeup people, set designers, permits, catered food, music, and so forth. *The Blair Witch Project*, shot in eight days by the actors themselves, was considered extremely low budget and reportedly cost around $35,000 to make.

The good news for low-budget filmmakers is that the commercial marketplace, which once had strict distribution and sales patterns and was difficult to break into, is much more open to independent productions. In a trend that began in the late 1980s with movies such as *Sex, Lies, and Videotape, Do the Right Thing,* and *Drugstore Cowboy,* audiences have developed a great interest in films made outside the studio system. In fact, they are so much in demand that they are now being released during the summer, a slot once reserved for action films. Big-name stars are even taking pay cuts so they can be a part of more meaningful projects.

Today there are more venues and festivals than ever catering to independent movies. Although most professional movies are still shot on 35mm film, the audience is becoming more accepting of digital video as a medium, thanks to movies like *Dancer in the Dark* and *28 Days Later.*

Another promising sign for newcomers is the expanded cable television market and the increasing number of direct-to-video productions. All of these trends mean that more films are being made—for more and different markets—than ever before.

What does this mean for the job market? More specifically, what does this mean for your chances of a film career? To understand what these developments mean to the film production industry, let's review for a moment just how a film is made.

Making a Film—Who Does What?

Film is a collaborative art. Although we speak of Steven Spielberg films, Ang Lee films, or Spike Lee films, we must not forget the large numbers of people who work behind the scene and even in front of the camera to make the film.

Whether a crew is making a feature film, a documentary, a commercial, or a television or video production, many of the job descriptions are essentially the same. They may vary slightly, depending on where the picture is being shot and which union rules apply.

There are several websites and books containing detailed job descriptions for the film and video industry. One comprehensive book is *Job Descriptions for Film, Video, and CGI*, by William E. Hines. *Career Opportunities in Television, Cable, Video, and Multimedia* is another good job directory. You will notice that film jobs can be divided into three categories:

- **Preproduction.** The planning phase, which encompasses a range of activity including budgeting, scheduling, casting, set and costume design, location scouting, set construction, and special effects design.
- **Production.** The "lights, camera, action" of Hollywood legend, when the cameras roll and the ranks of cast and crew swell sometimes into the hundreds and beyond. Production can take as little as one day in television, or as much as several months or more in film.
- **Postproduction.** When activity moves from the set to editing rooms, scoring stages, recording studios, and laboratories, where the project is shaped and molded into its final form.

Basic Jobs in Filmmaking

Space is too limited in this book to describe all the jobs that would be listed in a job almanac. But here are some of the major jobs and steps involved in making a film.

Scriptwriter

Every film begins with an idea. For instance, *The Worst that Could Happen*, a thirty-three-minute USC student film, could be reduced to this synopsis: "John loved being a player . . . but now he wants out of the game." The five-minute USC student film *Lone Star over China* is "an animated short in which a Chinese foreign exchange student finds a new way to live in his homeland after a year of study in Texas."

Turning these basic plots into complete films is the scriptwriter's job. Scriptwriters create a shooting script that not only gives the action and dialogue of the actors, but also indicates what the camera sees.

The idea can come from several sources. Often the scriptwriter with a story to tell works out the script or outline and attempts to sell it. Sometimes the idea originates with a producer, who then hires a writer (or several writers) to develop the idea into a script. Sometimes a producer or a production company buys the film rights to a book or stage play or to an individual's story of an especially dramatic event. Then a scriptwriter is hired to convert the idea into a screenplay.

Producer

The producer often raises money to finance the film and organizes staff and facilities for production. He or she may work with a production manager or assistant director who estimates the cost of the film and breaks it down into a budget, determining the most efficient way of shooting. The producer often works with the director and casting director in negotiating with and selecting actors and actresses. Generally, the producer is responsible for business transactions.

In film there may be line producers and an executive producer. Although they both share the ultimate financial responsibility for the success or failure of a film or television production, the line producer is more intimately concerned with the nuts and bolts of the production. How much of the creative responsibility he or she shares is often negotiated with the director and can vary from project to project.

Film has been called "the director's medium;" television is often thought of as "the producer's medium."

Director

The role of the director, who is primarily responsible for the creative vision of the completed project, is extremely important. Even though the director also may serve as producer and/or writer, he or she is still classified as a director—with all the rights and responsibilities that have been negotiated for that role.

In general, it's the director's job to translate the written script into what you see on the screen. That usually involves much of the prefilming preparation, as well as the actual production. It is the director who decides how scenes will be shot and guides the actors and actresses.

After filming, the individual scenes are assembled. Substantial technical work on sound, color correction, and music scoring is necessary before the finished picture is ready for release. The director is responsible for the presentation of his or her cut of the motion picture. In fact, the director's assignment is not complete until he or she has presented the director's cut to the employer.

On feature films, there are often first and second assistant directors. There is usually a continuity person, often called a script supervisor, who makes notes on each take and writes down comments the director may dictate.

Production Designer

Before filming starts, the director consults with the production designer, who designs the physical look of the film. Riggers, carpenters, painters, and laborers are assigned to build sets. The physical look of the film involves a wardrobe designer, makeup artists, a hairdresser, lighting, special effects, location scouts and props people, and set decorators.

For a motion picture involving a limited number of locations and sets, the production designer's job is relatively easy. For a big-screen spectacle, such as *Gangs of New York* or *Lord of the Rings*, which is shot in several locations, the production designer's responsibilities are enormous.

Actor

Actors entertain and communicate with the audience through their interpretation of dramatic roles. Only a small number achieve recognition in motion pictures or television. Many are cast in supporting roles or as walk-ons. Some start as background performers with no lines to deliver. Also called "extras," these are the people in the background—crowds on the street, workers in offices, or dancers at a ball. Others perform stunts, such as driving cars in chase scenes or falling from high places.

Although a few actors find parts in feature films straight out of drama school, most support themselves by working for many years outside of the industry. Most acting jobs are found through an agent, who finds auditions that may lead to acting assignments.

Cinematographer

The director of photography, often called a cinematographer, heads the camera section. He or she consults with the director and organizes placement of cameras and lighting. The director of photography is responsible for the quality of the photography. Although the cinematographer checks the framing of the take through the viewfinder of the camera, he or she does not operate the camera. That's the job of the camera operator.

Camera operators handle all camera movements and perform the actual shooting. Assistant camera operators check the equipment, load the camera, operate the slate and clapsticks (now electronic), and take care of the equipment.

Sound engineering technicians, film recordists, and boom operators record dialogue, sounds, music, and special effects during filming. Sound engineering technicians are the "ears" of the film. They supervise all sound generated during filming. They select microphones and the level of sound from mixers and synthesizers to ensure the best sound quality. Recordists help set up the equipment and are in charge of the individual tape recorders. Boom operators handle long booms with microphones that are moved from one area of the set to another. Because more filming is done on location and the equipment has become compact, lighter, and simpler to operate, one person often performs many of the above functions.

Multimedia artists and animators create the movie "magic." Through their imagination, creativity, and skill, they can create anything required by the script, from talking animals to flaming office buildings and earthquakes. Many begin as stage technicians or scenic designers. They not only need a good imagination, but also must be part carpenter, plumber, electrician, and electronics expert. These workers must be familiar with many ways of achieving a desired special effect because each job requires different skills. Computer skills have become very important in this field. Some areas of television and film production, including animation and visual effects, now rely heavily on computer technology. Although there was a time when elaborate computer animation was restricted to blockbuster movies, much of the three-dimensional work being generated today is happening in small and midsized companies. Some specialists create *synthespians*—realistic digital humans—that appear mainly in science fiction productions. These digital images are often used when a stunt or scene is too dangerous for an actor.

Many individuals get their start in the industry by running errands, moving things, and helping with props. Production assistants and grips (stagehands) are often used in this way.

Editor

After the film is shot and processed, film and video editors study footage, select the best shots, and assemble them in the most effective way. They work closely with the director to achieve the artistic effect the director wants. Their goal is to create dramatic continuity and the right pace for the desired mood. Editors first organize the footage and then structure the sequence of the film by splicing and resplicing the best shots. They must have a good eye and understand the subject of the film and the director's intentions. The ability to work with digital media is also becoming increasingly important. Strong computer skills are mandatory for most jobs. However, few industrywide standards exist, so companies often look for people with skills in the hardware/software they are currently using.

Today the lines between film and videotape are no longer as sharp as they were when television first began. Scenes shot on film are transferred to videotape for ease in editing, and the finished product can be transferred back to film, if desired. Often, outside postproduction houses are engaged to handle the technology involved in these transfers.

Assistant editors or dubbing editors select the sound track and special sound effects to produce the final combination of sight and sound as it appears on the screen. Editing room assistants help with the splicing, patching, rewinding, coding, and storing of the film.

Sound and music editors also work on the film. Though dialogue and sounds recorded during shooting are taped, they are only a part of the final sound track in the finished production. Much of the sound, as well as the music, is added in the postproduction phase, which is where sound and film are synchronized and "married." This type of work is increasingly computer driven.

When the Film Leaves the Studio

Whether it was made by a studio or acquired by a distribution company, once the film is ready to go and the appropriate personnel who approve it have signed off, copies are printed, distributed, and sent to exhibitors for showing. Studios keep tight control on their films, since pirated copies may cost them thousands of dollars. For instance, Toronto police, working with the Film/Video Security Office of the Canadian Motion Picture Distributors Association, seized illicit video copies of *Batman*. The movie theater at which the taping was allegedly made was identified through a "fingerprinting" system Warner Bros. used on each of the four thousand worldwide theatrical 35mm prints of the film. The encoded serial marks can be detected in all pirated film-to-video and subsequent video-to-video transfers.

Emerging Fields

Due to the nonstop advances in filmmaking and exhibition technology, new types of jobs are created constantly, especially in the new media, like the Internet and interactive, high-definition television.

In some areas of the film industry, new technologies are creating job openings faster than qualified candidates can be trained. Computer animation is a case in point. Thanks to the popularity of films like *Toy Story* and *Finding Nemo*, the major studios started investing heavily in computer-animation projects, and now it is a major part of the industry, with computer animation being used in live-action movies as well.

The job you hold in the film industry may not even have been invented yet! But one thing is certain: You stand a better chance of getting it if you keep up with industry developments and needs.

More Than Just Movies

The term *film*—as it is used in this book—encompasses a great deal more than theatrical motion pictures. That's good for jobs and good for you! If you've been thinking of "film jobs" as just those related to motion pictures you see in a theater, you need to broaden your scope. Today film can encompass broadcast and cable television, made-for-TV movies and miniseries, commercials, music videos, corporate television, video streaming on the Web, and much more.

The TV Effect

Whether you go to the movies frequently or not, chances are you are much more knowledgeable about the moving image than you realize. That's because you've almost certainly been a part of the television generation and have grown up accepting television as part of your everyday life. According to the U.S. Census Bureau, as of 2002, 98 percent of the nation's households have at least one television set. Cable television has been expanding at an amazing rate. In 2002 more than sixty-nine million people subscribed.

Today's filmmakers do not expect to receive all their revenue from the money they're paid by theater exhibitors, either domestically or internationally. Often the sale or rental of videos and DVDs brings in a substantial amount, as well as licensing to television broadcasters and Internet video-streamline services.

Since the introduction of VCRs in the 1970s, moviemakers and moviegoers have gone through some changes. For one thing, fewer people are going out to the movies. More households than ever own a VCR, and staying home to watch movies is a popular choice. In the 1970s only 1 percent of television households owned a VCR; by 1988 the figure was 58 percent; by 2002, 85 percent. Now the popularity of DVD players, with their high-quality images and bonus features, is on the rise.

How has Hollywood been handling the shift? One response is increased ticket prices. According to Exhibitor Relations, box office revenues are up in Hollywood, despite the dwindling audiences, because ticket prices have increased substantially. The other way moviemakers have handled the shift to the small screen is to produce more for the direct-to-video/direct-to-Internet market. These motion pictures, intended for home viewing rather than commercial release, are changing and expanding the opportunities in film.

The Corporate World

Films provide more than just entertainment, and the motion picture industry extends beyond the local movie theater and video store. Many films are designed to teach a variety of subjects from exercise videos to corporate training films. Corporate, or industrial, filmmaking is another large branch of the industry, and one that is easier for most beginners to enter. Corporate filmmakers may work for a video production house that produces a variety of educational tapes, or they may be self-employed scriptwriters or producers hired to create a film that is tailor-made to fit the needs of a specific corporation.

Wherever they work, corporate filmmakers go through the same process and face many of the same challenges tackled by those who create feature films. Whether your "star" is Vin Diesel or the latest piece of industrial equipment, the first thing you need is a script. Chapter 3 explains more about scriptwriting and the entire process of preproduction.

3

PREPRODUCTION

GOOD FILMS AREN'T just made. They're scripted, cast, and produced, and much of the work is done on paper before the cameras start rolling. This planning and "paperwork" stage is called preproduction. It's the time when all the details are considered: fine-tuning scripts, finding funding, establishing budgets and production schedules, considering locations, and selecting cast members. Many professionals contribute to the preproduction stage—too many to list here. Writers, directors, and producers do most of the work. Production managers, production designers, and location scouts are hired along the way to assist in the planning.

Scriptwriters

Scripts originate in different ways. Sometimes a writer with a good idea completes and sells an original movie script. Sometimes a producer seeks out writers to transform a story concept into a finished script. Plots for scripts may be fictional. They may be based on a novel, a play, or a comic book. They may be based on true events. Whatever their original inspiration, scriptwriters are the ones who face the blank page.

It can take several months to complete a screenplay. It can take years. Most scripts progress through stages and undergo substantial revision; they are seldom the work of one person. Often the first stage is not a script at all but a short synopsis of the idea, a concept that writers use to sell their stories. A concept distills the plot of a movie into several sentences or several pages. A slightly longer version, used for the same purpose, is called a treatment. Some scriptwriters use concepts or treatments to pitch their idea to a producer or a studio. If the idea sparks interest, they transform the treatment into a full-length script. Of course, if a producer has already hired them to develop a script or adapt a novel or play, they begin work on the existing plot.

Whether they work alone or with a partner, scriptwriters are team players. The script they complete may be adapted before or during production by directors, producers, or studio executives. Once shooting starts, actors may request changes in dialogue or directors may need to have scenes slightly or radically revised as the movie takes shape. Scriptwriters must be willing to accept these changes gracefully to succeed. Those who can't accept changes to their work either leave the business or try to become producers themselves, so that they can bring their original ideas to the screen with fewer changes.

In television, writers usually work in teams of several people who must agree on a story line and characters for each episode and the program in general. They work with strict budgets and deadlines to be met. Writers are often hired to work on reality television shows and documentaries, to write the narration and help organize the ideas to be presented. In these situations, they may not be involved until the postproduction stage.

Job Opportunities

Scriptwriters are an elite group. The Writers Guild of America, West estimates that 3,524 people worked as television writers in 2001; another 1,870 were employed as screenwriters. Although the guild has almost nine thousand members, just over half report income in any given year. So the number of writers earning steady income in the television and film industries is quite limited.

The field is currently experiencing slow growth. Approximately the same number of writers were employed in 1999, 2000, and 2001, slightly fewer than in 1998, the highest employment year on record. Screenwriting is growing faster at the moment than opportunities in television.

Salaries

Although their ranks are slim, writers are earning more money than ever before. The average guild member makes approximately $87,000 per year, and Writers Guild of America members earned a combined total of $782 million in 2001. The high salaries of top writers demonstrate that Hollywood values a good script. Some well-known writers may even share in the net profits of the film, especially if they receive less than their usual fee at the start of the project. This sort of deal allows writers to share more fully in the risks and rewards of making the film.

A Daytime Television Writer

Claire Labine, former coproducer and cowriter of "Ryan's Hope," began her television-writing career as a staff writer on "Captain Kangaroo." When she and her family moved to Brooklyn and bought their first house, they needed money to fix the plumbing. "What about soap operas?" her agent asked. CBS hired her as a dialogue writer on "Where the Heart Is." When the head writers on the show resigned, she and Paul Mayer took over.

"Where the Heart Is" was canceled eighteen months later, but Claire and Mayer had been offered a development deal for a new serial about an Irish-American family that ran a bar across the street from a major hospital. They produced and wrote "Ryan's Hope" for five years—a time in which the show stayed near the top of the ratings and won the Writers Guild award each year.

Eventually the show was sold to the ABC network, but it remained on the air for another nine years and Claire returned as head writer for the last eighteen months, so that she could make sure the show would end "in good form."

"Daytime television writers are hired in thirteen-week or twenty-six-week cycles," she explains, "and are usually paid a regular salary. On a one-hour show, the head writer is responsible for shaping the story line into daily episodes. These are assigned to associate writers, who write the outlines for each day's episode; and then to dialogue writers, who write the dialogue for each script."

Labine has advice for aspiring writers. She suggests that they even take a job sweeping floors, if necessary, to get in. "Over the years at 'Ryan's Hope,' we had a series of talented people—'golden gofers'—who eventually became staff writers. They had access to the outlines, the scripts, the daily taping, the cast, and the crew. They were able to assimilate the program's flavor and style. When they felt ready, they began writing scenes and slipping them under my door. By the time the show went off the air," she says, "they had enough experience to go on to other projects."

Labine also has this to offer: "Write, write, write. Every day. All the time. Don't spend a lot of time talking about writing. Save your energy for your work.

"Trust yourself. Listen to yourself. Write what moves you, no matter what other work you are writing.

"Take classes and seminars. Spend your time making friends with writers and producers. Cultivate a degree of emotional maturity; in this business there's a lot of ego. If you can't take criticism with a chuckle, you're dead."

Labine suggests contacting Writers Guild of America for a list of shows that accept submissions. Though locating an agent to handle your work is difficult when you're just breaking in, she says, "If you have a couple of pieces of good work, an agent will be glad to take you on. But don't expect an agent to find you work—you've got to network and do your part."

Labine believes more jobs for entertainment writers will open up in the next few years. "Opportunities are expanding," she says. "The dominance of networks in television is less; the dominance of major film studios has weakened because of independent productions and cable."

A Screenwriter

A veteran screenwriter, teleplay writer, novelist (*Take What You Will*), off-Broadway playwright, and short story writer, George Malko has more than a quarter-century of experience in freelancing since he left CBS News, where he worked on documentaries. Malko's background also includes receiving a UNESCO grant to help develop educational television in Australia; and writing, producing, and directing a documentary film there. He's received a grant from the National Endowment for the Arts to work on plays and was awarded the first Guggenheim Fellowship ever presented in screenwriting.

Malko's feature films include *Alien Thunder, Dogs of War, Luna, Sweet Lorraine,* and *Out Cold,* which he wrote in collaboration with Leonard Glasser. He finds a significant difference between screenwriting and fiction.

"Filmwriting and television writing are structural. Writing a novel affords you the luxury of moving in and out of time, in and out of your conscious or subconscious, as necessary. But you can't do that in film or television successfully, unless you explain each time—in a certain way—that you're going to do it. To be an effective screenwriter, you must follow the required structure. Enroll in a playwriting or screenwriting course if you need to learn the form."

His recommendation for would-be screenwriters: "Write a screenplay or teleplay. At the very least, try to write an episode of one of your favorite series, telling a new story, rather than merely retelling an episode that impressed you. What you've done can become your calling card.

"When you send your screenplay to a television program or film producer, it will probably be read by a reader," Malko tells his students. "Their job is to look for good new material. Without new ideas, or new versions of ideas, there would be no business."

If you do have a first-time writing experience for a first-time producer, Malko says, Writers Guild of America can advise you how to protect your material and how to make sure you are being paid what you should be paid.

Writers need to be realistic about the time it takes to get something read, he suggests. Six months is not uncommon; longer is not unknown. If you do work with an agent, Malko says, your most important responsibility is to communicate your dreams directly and honestly. If an agent does not know what a client wants to end up doing, the agent cannot offer effective professional guidance.

When an agent knows what you hope to do, the opportunity to work on a project can be weighed against the most important questions: Should you do it because you need the money? Should you do it because it moves you in the right direction toward what you want to do?

Though a story can be told many ways, Malko says, some topics are more appropriate than others for certain media. "Television generally is better for telling stories about characters and how they interact, while feature films are usually better for telling about larger-than-life events. For instance, you'd use television to show one family surviving a flood but feature film to show the flood's hitting a town."

Television is a better medium for docudramas because it's much more personal. The docudrama can be about big events, like hijacking or natural disasters. But drama based on documentary truth must be reduced in size to be accessible at a more personal level.

He's blunt about how hard successful writers work. "No one is ever going to knock on your door, offering you a bag of money to write. No muse will appear out of the atmosphere and whisper inspiration. You've got to do it all yourself."

Those who do, however, will be more in demand than ever, he believes. That's because international coproduction has changed the foreign market, and cable systems now produce original material. "Because of those two factors, more and more producers desperately need good writers."

Corporate Scriptwriting

In addition to the opportunities for writers in television and feature film, there is great demand for writers in the business world. Corporate scriptwriters create scripts to help their clients address issues within an organization. A corporate video may be designed to educate or motivate an audience; it may be designed to sell them something. Because the average corporate video is much shorter than a feature film, it generally has a narrow focus, usually communicating a single message with more emotional impact than the written word alone.

Scripts for corporate videos begin with a meeting between the writer and the corporate client. Sometimes the client has a clear idea of what message needs to be conveyed in the video; sometimes the client just has a general issue that needs addressing, such as poor employee morale. In the latter case, the client will look to the writer to investigate the issue, interview employees, and help define what the video's focus should be.

If the client is already clear about the message, the scriptwriter might start by interviewing experts in the field, doing original research, or reading and digesting written materials provided by the client.

Once this phase is finished, the writer decides on an approach and writes a treatment, a two-to-five-page summary of the creative concept. The treatment explains what techniques are planned for the video: animation, testimonials, or a video tour of the plant, for example. During the next two to four weeks, these ideas are fleshed out in various drafts of the script. Usually the scriptwriter will agree to provide a specific number of drafts. This not only provides the client with opportunities to respond to the script, but it also protects the writer from unlimited requests for revision.

Salaries

Some video scriptwriters work in-house in video departments. Many, especially since the restructuring common during the eighties, work as freelancers. For freelancers, there are three ways of billing clients. They may charge a percentage of the production budget, and the budget itself varies widely from several thousand dollars to more than $100,000. Other writers bill their clients according to the length of the finished video. Still others bill on a straight hourly rate. Appropriate rates vary according to region.

Video writers often belong to the Media Communications Association International (MCA-I) or to local video associations. These groups can provide more information about breaking into the world of corporate video.

Producers

Once the writers have finished a script, producers become involved. In some cases, the writer and producer is the same person. Producers have a large and complicated job, and much of it takes place during the preproduction process. Producers develop the budgets and schedules for feature films; they also hire many of the other people necessary to complete the project.

Most films are quite expensive to make, and the first step beyond the script is finding the necessary funding. In some cases, a studio, private investors, or the corporation that commissioned the film has already promised the money. Sometimes a star will purchase the film rights to a novel. In these cases, funding is assured. More often the producer, sometimes accompanied by the director, must raise funds for the movie based on the script.

How much money is needed depends on the script. A good producer is able to analyze a script and develop a budget for the movie. Of course, the budget may change once production is under way, but producers are valued for their ability to complete films on time and within budget. Some production costs are fairly standard: salaries for craftspeople, equipment, and location expenses. The largest and most variable expense is often the salaries of the leading actors and the director.

Once producers have financing for a movie, they can move forward with other aspects of preproduction, including scheduling. Based on the overall production schedule—the dates at which the film must reach each stage in the production process—the producer develops a shooting schedule. Usually the fastest and most cost-effective way to shoot a movie is to film it out of sequence. Most shooting schedules are based on locations. When the film crew arrives at a location, every scene that takes place there is filmed. Outdoor scenes are usually filmed first; indoor scenes are filmed later, once sets are completed, or when the weather doesn't permit the crew to work outdoors.

Deciding where to work and who to work with are two other aspects of the producer's job during preproduction. Scouting for locations is a task that the producer sometimes delegates, either to a production manager or to a professional company that finds locations. Sometimes the director rather than the producer selects the location. Regardless of who chooses the spot, the producer usually wants to look at it. Then the production manager and her/his staff can acquire the necessary permits and releases that allow the rest of the crew to go to work.

Selecting the cast and crew is another major aspect of preproduction, one that is usually controlled by the director with input from the producer. How are movies cast? It varies. For the leading roles, the writer, producer, and director often have people in mind. Then they must negotiate with those actors and their agents to gauge the actors' interest and settle on a fee. For smaller parts, a casting company may be used. The producer or production manager provides the casting company with a list of the types of actors needed.

Clearly producers pave the way for successful moviemaking through careful planning and attention to detail throughout the preproduction process. These behind-the-scenes details may not seem very creative or glamorous, but they are what allow producers, directors, and actors to create movie magic once the crew arrives on the set.

Opportunities

The growth of cable television, home movie rentals, direct-to-video productions, and the foreign market have expanded the number of opportunities for television and film producers. The field is expected to grow through 2005, which is good news.

The bad news is that because of the glamour associated with the industry and the potential for great earnings, the field of interested job candidates is crowded. Television and film producers face intense competition entering the industry. Once there, their success depends mostly on their reputation and track record. Lucky breaks come easiest to those with a solid education in film, hands-on experience at any level, and a willingness to be persistent.

Salaries

Film and television producers' salaries vary widely and have more to do with the art of the deal than with minimum rates negotiated by the guilds. Complicating things further is the fact that many producers receive a share of the net profits, either in lieu of or in addition to their fee for producing a project.

Television producers may earn less than $100,000 per year, or they may earn tens of millions a year. Film producers negotiate their own deals with studios, and for those who are well known, the deals can be quite lucrative. Often a film producer is also the movie's director, so the producer's fee represents just a portion of his or her actual earnings.

Obviously the salary range is wide and depends on the producer's reputation, fame, and ability (aided by a lawyer or agent) to negotiate a good deal.

A Television Producer

Lara Stolman is a freelance documentary television producer. When she graduated from college, she knew she wanted to work in film or television but was not sure in what capacity. So she got a job in the feature development department of a production company in Los Angeles. When she moved to New York City, she found that development jobs were scarce. Since she was interested in documentaries, she took a position as an executive assistant in the HBO documentary department. This gave her the opportunity to meet documentary filmmakers and learn the business. Once she felt ready, she started proposing and developing projects for the company. After two years she left HBO to work in documentary production. She became an associate producer, and then a producer, working mostly on hour-long programs for a variety of networks, from VH1 to MSNBC to the BBC.

"Being a producer means something different in film than it does in television. It means something different in documentaries than in does in newsmagazines. When I'm hired to produce something, I'm hired to produce, direct, and write." Lara's projects usually have a three-month schedule. She is provided with a subject matter and frequently a format. There's a research phase of a few weeks that culminates in a treatment. A production phase follows, which can involve mostly shooting but sometimes is more of a search for pre-existing footage or materials that can be licensed and used. Then her team logs every piece of footage (if there's dialogue it is transcribed). Lara writes a script and finally puts the show together with an editor.

To be a television documentary producer, Lara suggests you will need skills usually acquired in college. "For the most part, you will be expected to write, and you will be expected to write well. You will be expected to have a strong sense of dramatic structure. You need to be able to manage other people as well as a budget. It's good to have an interest in current events, culture, et cetera. And I think it's important to be able to make people feel comfortable with you, so you can enable them to tell their story."

Lara has also noticed a trend toward television producers doubling as editors and camera operators, which has made the job more complex. "It's helpful to have an understanding of certain technical aspects of filmmaking. If you know how to shoot a camera, you'll have a great advantage."

Many television producers change jobs regularly. Lara has worked for companies on staff, but more often she is hired as a freelancer to work on specific projects. This allows—in fact, requires—the flexibility to work on many different kinds of productions. "The great thing about freelancing is that you get to work with lots of different people. There is a lot of creative freedom and opportunities for growth. It might be easier to rise through the ranks if you're a freelancer than if you're on staff."

The downside is that Lara is always on the lookout for her next job. What's her strategy? "It's all word of mouth for me. I have a network of people that I've built over the years and stay in touch with. When I'm about to become available, I call them and ask them if they know of any jobs."

Lara advises freelance producers to join professional organizations and participate in their activities as a way of nurturing new relationships; this may come in handy when you're job hunting as well as when you're preparing a project. But most important, she says, is to "be flexible."

Other Preproduction Jobs

The director and producer cannot prepare a project for production by themselves. Although the final decisions in casting are made by the director and/or the producer, the job of finding appropriate actors, including extras, for all the various parts in a project is usually left to a casting company or director. This job requires prescreening actors, defining the qualities the part requires, selecting a number of actors who fit the role, arranging for auditions, and either choosing an actor or recommending the best to the director for consideration. The casting company or director also negotiates the contracts with the actors who are hired.

Most casting directors learn their trade through informal apprenticeship, and many work as freelancers, hired by film and theater productions or advertising agencies for specific projects. Some casting directors work as staff for studios or television networks.

Similarly, the location scout is the person responsible for finding locations for specific scenes in a film. They location scout does not simply search for the best, most beautiful spots that reflect the director's vision. Often budget and permission issues are involved. Appropriate locations need to be available, practical, and affordable. The scout will usually present several options to the director and producer, including information regarding required permits, accessibility of services, how other businesses will be affected by the crew's presence, and so forth.

The process of set design begins very early. The set designer works with the director and cinematographer to define the style of the film. Then she/he does research, designs, and supervises the construction of sets, taking into consideration the budget as well as the expressive and technical requirements (such as lighting) of the project.

Every prop and window view is ultimately the responsibility of the set designer, who must know how to sketch and paint as well as have an understanding of construction and materials.

Meanwhile, the costume designer works with the hair and makeup artists (and the director and actors) to create the right look for each particular character. A character's clothing should reflect the time period as well as the personality within the context of the film, so the designer must pay attention to details.

Sometimes a costume designer creates all the garments from scratch. Sometimes the process involves a hunt for existing articles that you might expect the character to own. Like the set designer, the costume designer must be aware of budget and technical issues and be able to work as part of a collaborative team.

4

Production

AT LAST IT happens. With the script polished, crew hired, and budget approved, the time finally comes for the crew to assemble for the first time and begin to make the film or television show. This middle phase of the process, when the work most familiar to outsiders gets done, is known as production. Although a countless number of people contribute to the success of the production phase, we will focus on two sets of professionals whose work is especially crucial: directors and cinematographers.

Directors

We all know who the director is: the person who starts and stops the action on the set with the magic words "action" and "cut." However, few of us realize how extensive the director's job is at every stage of production. Most directors are involved in a film from the development of the script through the publicity tours.

Directors are involved with script development in several ways. Some directors enter the field because they write and they want the freedom to bring their own scripts to the screen. Others, especially well-known directors, receive unsolicited manuscripts that they review themselves or with the help of hired readers. Even when the director doesn't write or select the script, he or she still influences the script by meeting with writers as the script takes shape and by requesting revisions as needed at any point from preproduction through final editing.

During preproduction the director is busy assisting the producer with things like scheduling, casting, location scouting, and budgeting. Directors help producers estimate the budget for a film by assisting with the creation of the "breakdown," which lists the anticipated expenses scene-by-scene. Expenses, in turn, are determined by factors such as the amount of time and number of extras needed for a given scene and whether the scene will be shot on location or require the construction of a special set. As the film proceeds, the director also may help the producer find ways to trim the budget when proposed costs are higher than the studio would like.

Before the cameras roll, directors also spend time hiring the crew and carefully investigating their reputations and references. Additionally, directors scout locations and discuss the "look" of the film with the cinematographer.

Once filming starts, directors do what they are best known for; they rehearse the actors and shoot the film. This stage, of course, also requires some planning. Directors develop a "shot list," a written plan of what to shoot, from what angle. They may create storyboards for sequences that are large-scale or require expensive equipment to shoot. Some directors plan every shot and rehearse extensively, as Alfred Hitchcock did. Others like to have a looser system that allows for some spontaneity. Whatever the system, all directors face the unpredictable: from sudden changes in the weather to sudden requests from studio management to cut the budget or shorten the shooting schedule.

When they have finished shooting the film, directors still have miles to go before their job is completed. First, they review the "dailies" with the film editor to select the best "takes" and to help the film editor begin to assemble the film. This process may take weeks or months and may involve cutting scenes, moving scenes, or even filming a new scene.

In addition to editing, the director spends a substantial amount of time during postproduction working on the sound of the movie. Directors supervise postsynchronization or "looping," during which actors create voice-overs or new dialogue in a sound studio. ADR—computer-assisted automatic dialogue replacement—speeds this process.

Next, directors work with the composer. They first meet to discuss the music for the movie in detail, so the composer can create a master log that documents the director's preferences for each scene. Then the composer creates the score. When it's ready, the director attends scoring sessions where musicians—often a full orchestra—perform the score on a sound stage.

Directors also help sound editors fine-tune the background noise in each scene to create the right final sound mix: the perfect blend of dialogue, music, and special effects.

Similar fine-tuning proceeds with the visual aspect of the film. The director and cinematographer collaborate to correct the density (light/dark balance) of the film. They also adjust the color balance of the print, playing with a range of warm (red) to cold (blue) that is ultimately highly subjective.

When the last bit of postproduction work is finished, the director steps in to help with marketing the movie by offering assistance with the creation of the movie trailer or taking off on a publicity tour.

Opportunities

Directors, like producers, often have a hard time breaking into the field; it's a glamour industry that continues to draw more interested newcomers than the industry can support. If you want to understand how many people dream of becoming a director, consider the competition for slots in the Directors Guild training program for assistant directors. Most years, between twelve hundred and two thousand people apply for the eight to twenty available openings.

How can you beat those odds? Getting your start in a local market or by making corporate videos or commercials may be easier than packing your bags and heading for Hollywood right away. Insiders say that educating yourself and making contacts is crucial. Often that means a willingness to take an entry-level job, such as working as a production assistant, to meet people and gain an important overview of the process. Being ready for those rare opportunities when they occur is the key.

More effective than working your way up the assistant director ladder might be to get experience by working on your own projects, directing short films to send to festivals and building a reel that shows producers what you are capable of.

Salaries

It is difficult to generalize about what directors earn because so many factors influence their pay. Some directors work on salary and are steadily employed; others offer their services on a freelance basis and are employed more sporadically. Often the director is also the producer, and that, too, influences the figure. Further complicating things is the fact that directors, like actors and writers, are usually entitled to residuals—fees collected each time a completed project airs another time. Sometimes the director's salary is based on union minimums; sometimes the director is a big name with a multimillion-dollar contract with the studio.

The minimum rate for members of the Directors Guild of America (DGA) directing a high-budget feature is $12,969 a week, while the rate for low-budget features is $8,150 a week. But most movie directors expect to make more than the minimum rate, and well-known directors receive millions from the major studios.

Television directors get paid according to the length of the program. The DGA minimum for a half-hour network prime-time show is $18,889 (with seven guaranteed days of work). For a half-hour cable television show the rate is $8,005 (six guaranteed days of work). Again, this is the minimum. The daily rates are higher: $3,373 a day for a prime-time network show, $1,668 for cable.

Producers/Directors

In the corporate video environment, meeting a company's objectives involves knowing how to do the following: work with people inside and outside the organization; refine an often-hazy concept into a crisp, clean script that clearly portrays the desired ideas; and, above all, accomplish all this within a tight, no-frills budget.

Chris Bone, a University of Southern California graduate who majored in production in USC's Department of Cinema, gained experience in the field as Producer/Director II at Home Savings of

America, the largest savings and loan institution in the United States. He says: "In corporate film and video, you're not seeing the same money or time it takes to do projects, or the same resources necessary to polish your work, that you see as the normal pride of craftsmanship in the feature film industry. In corporate video, the emphasis always has to be on the bottom line. The whole infrastructure of corporate video doesn't give you the margin of error you have in the entertainment world. You have to do things—create effects—with the budget in mind. You can't take actors to Siberia. You can't afford the time to give them the mindset you want.

"Even in the most expensive commercials, they can build in time for developing routines and rehearsal time. There's money for special lighting. Directors can be selective—can shoot a scene several ways and pick what they like. That's not generally true in corporate video. Money and time are just too tight. Instead, corporate video effects are usually created in the conceptual stage, rather than in the actual production. You've got to know what can be done, and how to do it economically.

"As a director of corporate video, you've got to motivate your people to put in the creativity that you don't have money to buy. You want top quality, and you'd like to come out with an entertaining product. Entertainment is great if it happens, but most of the time, it won't. Your job is to produce the film or tape that does the job for management."

Bone, who has considerable freedom in scheduling his work, often has busy days. They might start with research calls, finding out from clients (who are usually managers or department heads within Home Savings) what they really want to accomplish in the project they've commissioned. Some information may be sensitive, and Bone's job is to ask the right questions so appropriate material could be included or excluded in the final version.

The background work that is usually settled before Bone begins a project includes schedules, desired completion dates, and the maximum the client wants to spend.

"My job is self-supervising," Bone says. "I can create work for myself and others through my initiative in suggesting projects. I follow the company's management guidelines and general policies, but I manage people when I arrange shooting schedules and hire a crew."

Bone may write a script himself or commission a freelance writer for the project. "An outline takes anywhere from one hour to several days, depending on how creative or technical a particular project is and how much we need to organize the information," he explains. "A treatment (the next step) takes anywhere from a few hours to a week to write."

After the client approves the treatment, Bone writes, or commissions, a full script: "Corporate scripts take about three weeks to do because you don't always have enough information to make creative judgments. You have to go back to your client for details or research the project. I've done scripts that have taken eight to ten weeks to write because they dealt with extremely technical subjects. I've done others in a few days."

Bone believes that involving clients throughout the project's life cycle helps, since they know what they're doing and can approve each step.

"From concept to completion, you'll be making adjustments in each project based on what you can afford to do. You may have to shoot more, edit more, or rewrite the music. You may have to go back to the drawing board and redo your whole program. These adjustments are what take up 90 percent of the producer's time in corporate video. As a producer, you baby each project through to completion, making sure it keeps moving forward."

Extremely important, Bone says, is keeping up with technology. "If you don't know the equipment, it will haunt you," he says. "The people you hire don't necessarily know it either, and you have to sense when they are wrong."

For his projects, Bone hires outside freelancers, including actors and crew, but he generally edits himself. Sometimes he'll personally shoot sequences; mostly he's on location, directing.

Professional growth for Bone involves practicing on equipment; attending technical seminars and conventions, such as those offered by MCA-I or the National Association of Broadcasters; and reading the trade magazines.

Cinematographers

The cinematographer, also known as the director of photography, or DP, is responsible for everything that relates to the lighting and camera work on a film. Cinematographers have a profound effect on the mood of the film; with a painter's eye for light and color, they translate the tone of the script into the visual medium of film. By changing the focus, angle, or lighting of a shot, they can soften sharp edges or play up shadows, creating a romantic or harshly realistic world for the actors to inhabit.

Like every other member of a film crew, cinematographers begin their work by carefully reading the script. During preproduction they also meet with the director to develop an overall concept for the project. DPs also need to meet with set and costume designers because the designers' choices regarding sets and colors have immediate impact on the cinematographer's work.

In addition to creative planning, the DP has practical matters to attend to, including hiring a crew and selecting the necessary equipment. Union regulations prevent DPs from handling the camera themselves. Instead, they hire the crew that actually positions and operates the cameras. This group includes gaffers, key grips, camera assistants, and camera operators.

The DP may not operate the camera, but he or she does select the camera and the film stock. DPs also decide on camera positions and angles, determine exposures, and select lenses and composition for the camera operator.

Cinematographers collaborate closely with directors. Before they design the lighting, they watch the director rehearse the actors. Then they begin to organize the details of the photography—f-stops, light level, color level, and focus—with input from the director. Like directors, DPs sometimes use storyboards for large, complicated scenes or difficult special effects.

While the film is in production, DPs maintain quality control by watching the dailies. Later, during postproduction, they can fine-tune their decisions as they work with the director to adjust the density and color balance of the print, making sure that the film is picture perfect.

Opportunities

Opportunities to work as a DP are limited but growing slowly. Looking for work in commercials, cable television, or corporate video is a simpler way to start than setting your sights on Hollywood. Developing samples of your work will help open doors, so look for opportunities to complete short projects, either as part of a workshop or an internship.

Earnings

Exact figures on what cinematographers earn are difficult to come by. However, what is certain is that those at the top of their field have the opportunity to make a great deal of money. Like directors and producers, well-known cinematographers can earn millions, both because of their initial fee for the project and because they are sometimes given a percentage of the net profit.

As in other areas of the industry, those working in feature film earn the most, with television and corporate DPs earning less. DPs are highly valued in advertising and thus well paid, so creating commercials is something anyone interested in cinematography should consider. Television and corporate DPs also have the advantage, usually, of being on salary, whereas an independent cinematographer's income will be more sporadic.

These discrepancies in work situations create a wide range of earnings in the field, from those who might make several thousand per project to those who earn millions.

Other Production Jobs

Most people who work in film start out not as an assistant director or a set designer, but as a production assistant (in television sometimes called a runner). Being a production assistant (or PA) can mean many things. Production assistants often run errands, prevent passersby from making noise on the set, drive actors to the shoot, do administrative work, and so forth. Some production assistants work for specific departments. A PA working for the production design department might help build a set, shop for props, and help maintain the set continuity while a scene is being shot. This is a job that requires flexibility, attention to detail, and a positive attitude. PAs who show initiative are likely to get promoted to other jobs.

Another important job in production is that of the script supervisor. The script supervisor assists the director by helping maintain continuity. Since films are usually shot out of sequence, somebody must be responsible for checking that the actors are wearing the right costumes for each scene, props are returned to their original position for each take, and so forth so that everything looks the same from one shot to the next. The script supervisor also takes notes and creates a production log to help the editor locate specific shots.

The makeup artist on a film is part of the production design team. Makeup artists use makeup to make the actors look better, worse, older, younger, dead, and so forth. They collaborate with the hairstylist, costume designer, and actors to create the right look for each character. Makeup artists working on a science fiction project or a story in which the characters age may need to be very creative.

An essential department during the production phase is the electrical crew, which is made up of gaffers, best boys, and grips. The gaffer is the chief lighting technician; he or she works with the DP and is responsible for setting up lighting equipment to fit the needs of each shot. The best boy is the gaffer's assistant. The grip's job is to move and assemble production equipment on the set. Grips usually man the crane for the camera and its operator. Their boss is known as the key grip.

5

Postproduction

After the crew has packed up and left the set, the job of creating movie magic shifts to the editing room. There, editors start the long process of sifting through the work that was done in production; they rearrange and polish each scene to be sure that the best work is captured, putting shots together like a puzzle that will make sense once every piece is in. They must understand and be aware of the subtleties of moviemaking, including background noises on the sound track and continuity between scenes. This final phase of moviemaking, or postproduction, requires dedication to detail. Talented film and sound editors add the finishing touches that ensure the completed project is work that everyone involved can point to with pride.

Today most editing is done on computers (on programs like AVID, Final Cut Pro, and others) in three phases: off-line, online, and sound editing. In the off-line phase, the editor puts the elements of the film together. This is the phase in which images and sounds are chosen, played with, and decided upon. Current technology permits editors to easily move clips, add effects, and modify the sound so the editor can look at several options and add pieces as she or he goes along. The end result is a fine-cut, in which every frame is accounted for.

In the online phase, the editor, usually a different editor using a specialized computer, does color correction and fixes problems with the selected footage so that the final version contains the highest-quality images possible. Once that part is completed, a sound editor does the same with the audio, adding sound effects where needed and adjusting the dialogue and music. After that, the completed program can be output onto videotape. If a composite film print is needed, a lab will usually take care of it.

Film Editors

Editing to rough cut stages is usually done while filming is in progress. Key members from cast and crew may look at the rushes daily, after a film laboratory has processed each day's exposed film.

Film editors collaborate with the director (or in television with the producer) during postproduction to select the final images that will make up the film. They choose the best shots and decide upon the best arrangement for the shots. Therefore, their work affects the structure and pacing of the film. It also uncovers the best and worst in everyone else's efforts. If the writers have been redundant in creating dialogue, the film editor can help. If an actor has over- or underplayed a scene, the film editor can minimize the damage. A good film editor works behind-the-scenes to help the film realize its full potential.

Film editors don't just "cut" the film; they may add to it or rearrange it. One of their chief tasks is to give it continuity. Each take is different, the result of the way the actors moved to the way the cinematographer lit the scene or placed the camera. Matching each take to the next can be a challenge. But it's the film editor's job to make sure the film flows from moment to moment, while deleting any spots that don't represent an actor's or writer's or director's best work.

Film editors are responsible for other visual aspects of the film as well. They design, prepare, and/or approve any opticals, titles, or stock footage that gets used in a film. They also work closely with the sound editors to help fine-tune the sound track.

Film editors, along with directors, work on synchronizing the voice and sound tracks with the picture. Their preliminary work paves the way for sound effects editors, who complete the job. Film editors also must view composite "answer" prints for quality control and coordinate the work of sound and music editors.

Film editing is a creative, complicated, drawn-out process, and it's one of the many hidden keys to great film.

Opportunities

Only a few hundred editors work regularly in feature film. There are more opportunities in television and corporate video. As the market for cable programming expands, the number of jobs is expected to increase, but breaking into the field is still difficult for beginners. Most newcomers must be willing to take jobs that at first don't fully utilize their skills. Starting at the bottom does pay off for some, giving them an understanding of the process of film editing and putting them in the right place at the right time, which is so often the key to landing that first good job in film.

Salaries

Earnings for film editors are governed by the union minimums negotiated by the Motion Picture Editors Guild. The basic contract currently provides weekly salaries of about $2,000 to $2,500, with overtime after forty or forty-eight hours.

Assistants earn slightly less. An assistant editor working on a feature film can expect to earn about $28 an hour, or between $1,000 and $1,400 a week. An editorial apprentice may start at $16 to $22 an hour.

Sound Editors

Sound editors play on our emotions. They create suspense; they help set the pace and shape the mood of a film. It is a job that demands close attention to detail and extensive cooperation with the other professionals who work behind-the-scenes in film.

Under ideal circumstances, the job begins with collaboration between the director and the supervising sound editor. If time permits, they watch the film together and discuss the overall strategy for the film.

It is up to the supervising sound editor to ensure the quality of every sound on the final sound track, with the exception of the music. Getting that job done means recording and editing all the natural and artificial sounds in the film. Sound editors use the Foley stage and ADR—automatic dialogue replacement—to make sure that everything we hear in the movie is distinct and authentic enough to draw us into the fictional world of the film.

Dialogue is at the forefront of what we hear in a film. Postproduction taping of dialogue, or "looping," is an important part of sound editing. However, sound editors also work to add background voices to the film. These voices must be just right, using accents and vocabulary that add to the reality of the scene.

In addition to working on ADR, sound editors spend a great deal of time on the Foley stage. There they re-create the sound in each scene, synchronizing the sounds of body movements with special effects and visual images. Footsteps can be re-created by "walking the Foley." Editors reproduce each step on a surface—wood, dirt, concrete—to create a sound that matches the onscreen action.

Sound effects technology has advanced greatly in recent years. Many sound editors also believe that the field is gaining new importance and increased respect from directors and producers.

Earnings

The Motion Picture Editors Guild negotiates minimum wage scales for sound editors. Currently those minimums stipulate weekly salaries of about $1,500 to $2,000 and hourly fees of about $35. Music editors earn similar amounts. Those who work overtime or are on-call are entitled to higher fees. As in other areas of the film and television industry, many sound editors earn more than the union minimums. However, their salaries and fees are much closer to the minimums than a well-known director or producer's earnings would be. In addition, sound editors tend to work as hourly or salaried employees and do not share in the net profits of the films they help to create.

Other Jobs

The postproduction supervisor is the manager of the entire postproduction phase. This is the person in charge of scheduling, budgeting, and making sure all the raw materials go to the right place. The supervisor makes arrangements with labs, recording studios, and equipment renters and makes sure that everything runs smoothly.

The film music composer creates the original music of a film: writing, producing, and orchestrating something that will match the themes of the story in all the various moods that the director hopes to create. A composer working on a film must be aware of all the other sound elements of the film and compose to the specifications of the director, rather than following his or her own inspiration.

The music editor (who may also be the music supervisor) does not write any of the music for the film, but rather works with the composer to shape the music into something that fits the pacing and the other sound elements of the film. The music editor is also involved in selecting prerecorded musical material for some scenes, and he or she may have to go through pieces of music from a music library as part of the job of coordinating the creation of the musical score.

The motion graphics artist or design team is hired to create the graphics and visual effects that are overlaid on the images. Any text seen on screen, as well as stills, color effects, logos, animation, and so forth, are usually the work of graphics artists. They use a variety of computer programs and must stay on top of the technology, as it evolves rapidly.

A Motion Graphics Artist

Dominic Amator is the art director and co-owner of Werkaround, a Manhattan production boutique that is often hired by film and television companies to handle the postproduction of their programs. Dominic is responsible for creating and/or overseeing the building of a graphic style for projects that come into Werkaround. With some projects he is involved from the beginning, collaborating with the clients to design a style for the show or film. Other times he is brought in to create specific visual effects (enhancing photographs or animating logos, for example) as needed.

What's the difference between motion graphics and special effects? "The line is blurry but special effects tend to be visuals (like a storm or a computer-animated character) composited into scenes as part of the narrative, whereas graphic elements for show packaging, quality enhancement, and style are usually considered motion graphics."

Dominic got his bachelor's degree in graphic design and a master's in interactive media. For people interested in pursuing special effects, he recommends focusing more on film production.

For the past few years the most useful programs to Dominic have been Adobe Photoshop, Illustrator, Adobe After Effects, and Discreet Combustion, but he is always interested in learning new ones, since software programs tend to adapt and overtake each other in their utility. "An important part of the job is to pay attention to media and deconstruct what you see so that you can learn to apply the new techniques to your own work."

Dominic's first job was at a corporate media production house, a good environment to learn in, he says, because he was able to get involved in creative decisions. After working on staff in a couple of postproduction houses, he and two editors decided to open a business so that they could all have more control over their careers and select projects that challenged them. Despite the risk and the extra work involved in running a business, Dominic enjoys being his own boss and the rewards of having satisfied customers.

To work in postproduction, Dominic suggests one needs to be able to contribute to the creative process but also remember that the purpose is to serve the director or producer. It's important to be resourceful and good at troubleshooting, both creatively and technically, since computers are so vital to the job. Projects are often behind schedule by the time they get to postproduction, so deadlines are tight and expectations can be unreasonable. But it's a good line of work if you want to spend a large proportion of your time on creative tasks.

6

Getting the Right Education

To work in film or television it is not required that you study film first. Many people who work in film acquire their craft on the job, and even if you have a postgraduate degree in film or television broadcasting, you will still have a lot to learn about professional production.

However, your education will determine what kind of jobs you will be eligible for. For some of the more technical jobs, you can prepare by taking technical courses. For most of the creative jobs, such as producing, writing, and production design, you will be expected to have a college degree.

If You Don't Go to College

Many jobs in film do not demand a college degree as much as a specific skill that may be acquired more quickly by taking shorter courses or certificate programs, or by working as an apprentice or intern. For example, if you want to work as a makeup artist or in costume design, you might be better off attending a professional school, since having a B.A. will not affect your job eligibility. You will be starting from the bottom anyway.

Many community colleges offer courses and degrees that are useful in film, such as audio engineering, electronics, carpentry, broadcasting, and so forth. These degrees can help you get in the door on film projects, and from there you can prove yourself to be a talented professional.

Also, most computer programs used in film, particularly in the computer-heavy field of postproduction, can be learned through nondegree course work and even independently. Although the depth of knowledge one gets in college is desirable, employers will be more interested in your portfolio or reel than in your academic training.

If You Do Go to College

There are no specific college or university courses you can take that will guarantee you an entry-level job in the film industry. No one even knows exactly how many film students there are, or just what they are studying. Most university film programs include courses in motion picture and/or television production, but some emphasize the study of film history or film criticism. Some universities have separate departments for film and television students. Other schools consider either theater or radio part of the same discipline. Some schools, in particular art schools, look at film as an art form, emphasizing its visual aspects.

Because film study means many different things to different people, you will have to consider what it means to you when you are choosing a college. It will take considerable research to find out what courses are offered and whether they seem to fit what you want to do with film. It is difficult to know what kind of an education would best suit you. If you know you want to be a screenwriter, you may be more interested in programs that allow you to focus on that. But there are also benefits to exploring the whole filmmaking process.

Spending an afternoon in your school or public library's reference department is a good way to start finding out what you're looking for. Film schools usually have websites that you can visit and gather up-to-date information on programs, class descriptions, admission requirements, and tuition.

One series of books you'll find helpful is the *College Blue Book*, a set of volumes that list degrees offered by college and subject. For example, it lists schools that offer undergraduate or graduate degrees in motion picture history, motion picture production, or motion picture technology. It is also available on CD-ROM.

Other books of interest are *College Rankings Exposed*, which may help you decide what criteria are important to you, and Peterson's *Undergraduate Guide to Four-Year Colleges and Film School Confidential*, a candid and detailed guide to M.F.A. programs that contains plenty of valuable suggestions for undergraduates as well.

Besides the type of program a school offers, you should pay some attention to its size and nonacademic offerings. Students at smaller colleges enjoy the individualized attention they receive from their teachers. However, larger schools may offer newer or more diverse production equipment, as well as a variety of extracurricular activities such as student-run campus television networks or radio stations, film clubs, and other organizations that could use someone with filmmaking skills. Be aware that a large university does not necessarily have a large film program. If you visit a campus, try to make time to look around the production facilities and find out what the students think about their program.

Location is another important consideration when you are choosing a film school. To begin with, do you know where you would like to live after you graduate? It will be easier to look for work if you live in the same town where you attended college, particularly right after you graduate. You will be familiar with the area, you will have built a network made up of colleagues and professors through your school, and maybe you will even have a former employer who can recommend you for more work.

Film and television have stronger production industries in some cities than in others. If you go to college in Los Angeles or New York, you may find larger professional communities, higher-end productions, and more internship opportunities. But in areas with less production there is also less competition and less pressure, which can mean more opportunities for growth.

Speaking of internships, the right internship could be the most important practical experience you have as a student. Does your school encourage internships? Are they part of the curriculum? Where do students typically intern and how involved is the school in helping them find the right place?

You want your internship to reflect your interests as much as possible, since it is where you will make the best connections and may be where you find your first job. Once you are there, remember that you are working for no pay, which means you should be getting an education as compensation. Volunteer for projects. Ask as many questions as you can. Get to know people doing the work you hope to do some day. Observe what people with entry-level jobs do and acquire those skills. Use free time to learn more about the company. Every day of your internship is a job interview, so treat it as a chance to impress your supervisor.

Getting Information

Once you've found several schools that interest you, write for catalogs and admission applications. Pay particular attention to the credentials of the faculty, which are usually listed in the bulletins. Are courses being taught by persons who are actually working in film, or have done so? Or are people whose primary interest is research and film criticism teaching them?

If possible, you will want to match your abilities and interests with a film department emphasizing areas you care about. However, you do not want to be so interested in production that you concentrate only on technical courses and neglect the rich heritage a background in, for example, film literacy can provide.

In a number of schools, you will not be admitted to a curriculum in film until you have completed one or two years of college courses in a variety of fields: literature, social science, math, and physical sciences. Don't let this discourage you. The additional maturity you gain from this waiting period, as well as the knowledge you acquire from the subjects you study, will almost certainly make you a better filmmaker. For instance, a documentary you produce on poverty or workers' conditions will be much stronger if you're familiar with *The Grapes of Wrath* or *The Jungle*.

You also may want to ask the department chairperson if he or she knows of alumni who currently hold jobs in the film industry. Realistically, only a small percentage is likely to be working in feature film. However, you should find alumni who work in related fields, such as corporate video, or who hold technical jobs.

Two cautions as you research schools and colleges: pay particular attention to deadlines and follow all application instructions. Admission to film classes is especially competitive, and the instructions on submitting your credentials are almost certainly inflexible. Some colleges will ask you to give them a personal statement about your goals in filmmaking and about yourself as a person. Take this request seriously. The quality of the statement you give them—in both the content and the competence of your writing—may be the factor that gets you in, or keeps you out.

Schools

You'll find colleges offering film courses in every state. Community colleges also frequently offer film studies or hands-on production classes. Enrolling gives you an idea of whether you really like film or video and want to make it your career. Following are descriptions of a few of the more prestigious schools. You will find their contact information in Appendix C.

California Institute of the Arts (CalArts)

The California Institute of the Arts, established in 1961, was the first degree-granting institution of higher learning in the United States created specifically for students of both the visual and the performing arts. Undergraduate film/video students choose concentrations in the following areas: live action, experimental animation, or character animation. M.F.A.s are offered as well, including one in film directing.

CalArts is highly competitive in admission requirements. In addition to high school (or college) transcripts, applicants for admission are judged on their talent and potential for successful professional study, as demonstrated by their portfolio, written statement of purpose, and production credits.

New York University

Under the Tisch School of the Arts, New York University provides undergraduate and graduate training in film, video, television, and radio; cinema studies; and dramatic writing. The undergraduate program combines professional training with a basic liberal arts education. Graduate degrees include the M.F.A. in film or dramatic writing and an M.A. or Ph.D. in cinema studies. The NYU School of Continuing Education offers nondegree courses and certificates as well.

University of California, Los Angeles

At UCLA, the undergraduate curriculum in film and television covers both theory and current technology. Students may study criticism, screenwriting, production, and animation. Study abroad and internship programs offer students further opportunities to learn about film and television.

Several advanced degrees are offered at UCLA. Students can pursue an M.F.A. in film/television production, screenwriting, or animation. An M.F.A. or Ph.D. in critical studies also is available. Admission to all these programs is extremely competitive. Certificate programs are offered for nondegree students.

University of Southern California

Founded in 1929, USC is the nation's first film school, and it remains one of the most famous. Admissions to the school, which offers both undergraduate and graduate degrees, are highly selective. The school offers extensive liberal arts education, including cinema and video history and theory, in addition to hands-on production experience at undergraduate levels.

Critical Studies Program

This comprehensive curriculum offers studies in two areas: film history, including world and Hollywood cinema and the history of film theory; or television and video history, particularly American broadcast television. Professors emphasize understanding a film or video in its historical and cultural context, its role in the development of film or television history, and how film and television shape the attitudes and values of their viewers. Programs leading to the M.A. degree and Ph.D. degree in critical studies are also offered.

Production Program

This two-year sequence includes specific instruction in camera, sound, editing, screenwriting, directing of actors, and directing of cameras. Students also have the opportunity to produce a school-sponsored major production in their senior year. Their films are screened at the USC Film Festival.

Filmic Writing Program

This four-year B.F.A. program allows undergraduates to practice the art of screenwriting with an emphasis on combining film form and film content. Students move from writing exercises to full-length fictional and documentary screenplays—from experimenting with nonverbal communication to integrating complex visual designs into advanced products. A two-year graduate program exists as well.

Peter Stark Motion Picture Producing Program

This full-time graduate program concentrates on the business aspects of filmmaking, including production, licensing, marketing, and distribution issues. Many Stark students enter with a prior degree in film or business. For those without production experience, a hands-on course is required in addition to other classes.

7

ON THE JOB HUNT

Now you know what kinds of jobs are available in film production. But how do you get them? There are thousands of film majors and television students currently enrolled in degree programs. Many people are competing for very few jobs in the glamorous world of feature film. What are your chances? How can you break in?

Film students may find help through their schools. Contacts acquired during an internship are an especially good source of job leads and often help aspiring filmmakers uncover the "hidden job market." Interns have a chance to acquire real-world skills and to become a known commodity to working professionals who can offer job leads, references, and, sometimes, even that first opportunity to work in film.

So it's important not to overlook the impression you make as a student. Are you on time for classes? Do you complete your projects on time? Do you participate in department events? Your faculty adviser may be asked about you. Have you developed a relationship strong enough to get you the reference you'd like to have?

Once you do have some experience, education, and a few professionals who will vouch for you, it's time to get serious about your job search. The film industry is competitive, so job hunters must be as proactive and as creative as possible in their search. These days technology can be a big help. The major studios now have websites that list current job openings. You can also post information about your credentials on the Internet so that anyone hiring in film can find you. Most film professionals agree that determination, patience, and luck are key ingredients in any successful career.

Getting the Experience

One recommended exercise for college students is to deliberately work on projects that have meaning beyond academic life. For instance, if you successfully shoot and complete a video program on training for a business firm, you will have something to show potential employers.

Volunteer to work at the campus radio, television station, or theater. Get experience in production, whether it is as a writer, on-camera talent, gaffer, stage manager, or some other relevant position.

Another way to gather experience, as well as money, is to set up your own video business, even while you're still in school. Offer to shoot family events like baptisms, bar mitzvahs, or weddings. People usually want a record of these events, and they'd rather pay a small fee for a quality video than leave it up to a family member to shoot.

Get as much hands-on experience as you can. Don't overlook the chance to do many things at a smaller television or cable station. In a smaller setup, you need to be able to recognize what has to be done and do it. If you show initiative, you may get the chance to produce a program. At the very least, your work will be appreciated.

One reason the hands-on experience is so valuable is that in production classes with large numbers of students, you may not have the opportunity for fieldwork (shooting and producing outside a studio setting). When looking for a job, you need to be able to demonstrate both that you have the experience and can edit—a chance you may not get if production classes are large.

Another useful skill to acquire while still in school is a sense of how business operates. Often, recent graduates don't have a real feel for the business world—they lack a certain sensitivity and knowledge, and this can hurt their chances of getting hired. Consequently any work experience is good to have on your résumé. Many entry-level jobs are administrative, so knowing how an office works as well as the computer programs used in regular business settings (such as Excel and PowerPoint) will be a desirable quality for job seekers.

Strategies

In film, nearly everyone is considered trainable for most jobs. Therefore, although experience is valued, employers pay a lot of attention to writing, oral communication, and interpersonal skills. If you can demonstrate that you have basic skills in production, editing, field production, scriptwriting, and the ability to consult with clients, you will be ahead of the game. In general, less interesting to employers is studio production experience, knowing how to operate and repair specialized equipment, and teleconferencing skills.

As a recent graduate the most valuable asset you can bring to a job application is a good reference, preferably from a professional the employer knows personally. A sample reel and a record of a successfully completed internship will help as well.

The bottom line is that when you're applying for work in film, *who* you know is more important than *what* you know. So actively pursue internships, even if they are nonpaid. Volunteer with professionals and be interested in their work. Try to make a good impression on everybody, because you never know who will lead you to a job, who will connect you to a future employer, who can give you the recommendation that makes a difference.

Sometimes, but not often, ads for jobs in the film industry are listed in general circulation newspapers or general job list websites (such as Monster.com and hotjobs.yahoo.com). Because it is usually easiest to start locally, and at the bottom, it is always worthwhile to keep your eyes open and read the employment ads in your local paper. This is especially true if you live in an area that is often used by filmmakers. You may find ads for film extras or production trainees. Opportunities in corporate video also may be uncovered through the want ads, especially if you live in an urban area.

If there is a company you're interested in working for, check out its website. It may have a help-wanted section. But don't wait for an ad to apply for work. Send the company your résumé. Try to get in touch with a person, maybe a production manager or a producer with hiring capabilities. Let this person know you would like to work for him or her. Be persistent.

Also, contact your local film commission. It will know what projects are being produced in your area and may help you contact potential employers. Once you have a job, you may be talking to the commission anyway.

Developing Your Reel

Early in your student life you should start saving samples of your work for your portfolio. Later, before job hunting, you'll select only your best and most professional work. Make sure you keep a final copy of everything: video projects, scripts, photographs, and so forth. You never know what employers might be interested in seeing.

Eventually, you will develop a reel to use as your job-hunting portfolio, a montage that's between five and fifteen minutes long of your best work (longer programs will not be watched in their entirety). Like a résumé, you may alter it depending on the job you are applying for. If you haven't given prospective employers a tape before the job interview, bring the tape along and offer to leave it with them. Depending on the format, you'll want to make arrangements to get it back. Nowadays, it is not uncommon to present reels on DVD. That way the prospective employer can choose what to watch and for how long to watch it. Your reel should have your most professional work on it, and your role in each segment should be clear. You do not want to take credit for work you didn't do.

Whatever It Takes

If you really want a job in film or video, you need to be willing to do anything to get in. That may mean starting as a runner, a messenger, or a gofer. Plenty of people in film and television today got their start in the mailroom. You should be willing to work for free, and you should try to keep in touch with everyone you meet. If you know what field you want to work in (sound recording, costume design, production management), let people know.

Once you've been hired and can demonstrate your capabilities in the job you've been hired for, you'll have a better chance entering the world of production. If jobs open up in your own company, you'll be eligible to apply. In fact, you'll know about them before they are advertised. If you use your job as a receptionist as an opportunity to learn how to edit, you employer will be encouraged to give you a chance.

Read trade publications cover to cover. Studying the ads will show you what qualifications are needed for various jobs. If you don't know the equipment or computer programs mentioned, then you know what you need to learn.

Here are addresses for some websites that contain job lists for film and video professionals. Take a look to see what kinds of jobs are available and what skills they require:

mandy.com
entertainmentcareers.net
productionhub.com
2-pop.com
mediabistro.com

Nonproduction Jobs

Once a film is completed, there is still a lot of work to be done. Many people are involved in finding the right place to show a program. If you have a head for business, one of these areas might be a good place to find a steady, entry-level job that will also give you the chance to meet people working in production.

For unknown filmmakers, the first stop once they have completed their film is usually a festival, where they hope a distributor will see their film and want to buy it. There are many different kinds of jobs at film festivals, although most of them are temporary. You could be involved in programming of films, guest services, the logistics of the festival (scheduling, print traffic), publicity, and so forth.

Not only are festivals a great place to network, if you work there, they can also be a great place to learn about the business of films, since you will be likely to meet filmmakers, buyers, critics, and others. And, of course, you will have great access to the newest films.

A film or television program is usually made by a production company that may or may not know where the program will be exhibited once finished. When the company has no exhibitor, the production company may find a distribution company to take on the responsibility of finding an appropriate venue (or venues) for the program. The job of the distributor is to sell programs to exhibitors, whether they are studios, movie theaters, or television networks. They try to match what they know buyers are looking for with what they have to sell. For example, a documentary distribution company might try to sell its documentary about whales to Animal Planet and its film about the construction of the Golden Gate Bridge to the History Channel.

In turn, television networks, studios, and movie theaters have departments responsible for acquisitions, that is, locating and licensing appropriate programming for their needs. It is often cheaper and safer for television networks and studios to acquire a finished product than to make the investment involved in producing something new that might not work out.

Marketing is involved throughout all of this. The marketing department estimates what the audience for a film will be and develops a strategy to help distributors, exhibitors, and consumers identify the product. Trailers, posters, affiliations with junk food products, and so forth are all part of marketing. Making a particular film stand out can be a challenging job in today's media-saturated world, and a creative job, too.

8

SEMINARS, ORGANIZATIONS, AND FESTIVALS

FILM SCHOOLS, PROFESSIONAL organizations, and film festivals offer a wide variety of opportunities for first-time filmmakers, from intensive workshops designed to help students develop their first sample to film festivals created to introduce newcomers to the industry. Here is a small sample of the better-known resources and venues for filmmakers.

American Film Institute

The American Film Institute (AFI) is an organization dedicated to the advancement and preservation of motion picture art. Among other things, AFI sponsors a variety of seminars, workshops, and public service programs, held at the AFI campus in Los Angeles and in cities throughout the United States. These programs are taught by top film and television professionals and provide the film and video community, the independent artist, and the general public a forum for exploring current artistic and technical issues.

Though topics and presenters vary, a typical set of programs includes workshops on:

- Screenwriting
- Directing
- Cinematography and production
- Digital video
- Interactive television
- 3-D modeling and animation
- Multimedia

AFI charges fees for these workshops and seminars, but AFI members receive discounts on selected seminars. Membership fees for the American Film Institute start at $50 per year and include a year's subscription to the American Film members' newsletter and access to the online AFI catalog of feature films. Members also are entitled to discounted tickets and passes to AFI events, and they have eligibility to vote for the annual "AFI's 100 Years in . . ." series.

You can join AFI online at afi.com.

Los Angeles Film School

The Los Angeles Film School offers hands-on production-learning programs ranging in length from six weeks to one year that are taught by film and television professionals in small classes and are geared toward preparing participants for professional work. Visit lafilm.com for more information.

New York Film Academy

This academy offers basic and advanced courses in hands-on film production. Workshops offer participants the opportunity to write, direct, shoot, and edit their own short films. Students study some of the basic concepts of directing, story, camera, lighting, sound, and editing.

Courses are short, lasting four to ten weeks, and provide students with an immediate opportunity to begin making films. More comprehensive nine-month-long programs are also offered. In addition to the main headquarters in New York City, the school has locations in London and Los Angeles and courses are offered in other cities such as Austin, Texas, Barcelona, and Prague. To find out more go to nyfa.com.

ABC Talent Development Programs

ABC Television has several fellowship opportunities for aspiring television professionals. The directors' fellowship, cosponsored by the Directors Guild of America (DGA), offers thirty-six weeks of paid training under the mentorship of DGA directors. Applicants with prior directing or film/video experience are preferred. The program actively recruits ethnic minority and/or women directors for half-hour, multicamera taped and filmed comedies. Similar programs exist for writers and for future managers. For information check out its website at abctalent.development.com.

The DGA also gives annual awards of $2,500 to eight minority/female student filmmakers a year. Information on how to qualify is available from either of the DGA's offices, in Los Angeles and New York.

Organizations

Besides unions, there are myriad professional organizations you can get involved with—national, international, or local. Membership in these organizations can give you the chance to meet other people in your field, build your network, stay informed about the industry, and support your professional community. Many of these industry association conventions feature seminars and workshops that provide a good place to get technical training in film and video techniques, as well as creating informal opportunities to meet men and women active in a variety of corporate organizations. Such industry contacts can be helpful when you're looking for jobs. Indeed, these associations often run job referral services for members during their conventions.

IFP

The IFP (Independent Feature Project) is a nonprofit organization dedicated to assisting independent filmmakers and distributors with resources and information. Year-round events include the IFP Market, where filmmakers can show their films to buyers; conferences; workshops; screenings of new works; and newsletters.

With chapters in Chicago, Los Angeles, New York, Seattle, Miami, and Minneapolis/St. Paul, IFP offers great networking possibilities.

For more information contact:

IFP/New York
104 West Twenty-Ninth Street, 12th Floor
New York, NY 10001-5310
ifp.org

Media Communications Association International

The MCA-I sponsors an annual conference, an annual video festival, and periodic workshops and seminars. The group is intended for those working outside of the broadcast area. Members include video scriptwriters, producers, directors, consultants, and operations managers. They have chapters all over the world.

For detailed information on MCA-I contact:

Media Communications Association International
1000 Executive Parkway, #220
Saint Louis, MO 63141
mca-i.org

International Communications Industries Association, Inc.

ICIA is an international trade association serving its members—companies and individuals representing fifty-six countries—by providing education, exhibition, and information services. Its workforce development program is designed to help people enter the audiovisual industry.

For more information contact:

ICIA
11242 Waples Mill Road, Suite 200
Fairfax, VA 22030
infocomm.org

National Cable and Telecommunications Association

The NCTA was founded in 1952 with the mission of giving its members a unified voice on issues affecting the cable and telecommunications industry. The NCTA hosts an annual trade conventional called the National Show.

For information contact:

National Cable and Telecommunications Association
1724 Massachusetts Avenue NW
Washington, D.C. 20036
ncta.com

Festivals

Film festivals have been growing in number and size at an amazing rate. Audiences welcome the variety and originality they offer, industry professionals consider them a key means of discovering new talent, and first-time filmmakers understand that they can launch a career. There are too many festivals to list here, but what follows are a few of the more popular ones. You can find out about others on the Internet or by watching for ads in the trades.

Sundance Film Festival

The Sundance Film Festival was created in 1985 to "recognize independent filmmaking in all of its diversity." It has been a major force in the industry, and success at the festival has launched numerous filmmakers. Some in the industry believe the festival has become too commercial now that independent branches of the major studios are allowed to enter films. Nevertheless, Sundance remains one of the most popular and prestigious film festivals in the country.

The festival includes a competition of American independent films. In addition to the grand prize, awards are given in specific categories, including scriptwriting and cinematography. A noncompetitive program screens both American independent and foreign feature films and short subjects.

For detailed information about the institute, the festival, and submission guidelines check out the website at http://institute.sundance.org.

IFP Los Angeles Film Festival

The IFP Los Angeles Film Festival is a very popular event showcasing American as well as international independent films. The 2003 festival screened about seventy-two features, sixty shorts, and forty-seven music videos selected from more than twenty-five hundred submissions. The festival does not have a market, but awards are presented to films under feature, short, and documentary categories.

For more information contact:

IFP Los Angeles Film Festival
8750 Wilshire Boulevard, 2nd Floor
Beverly Hills, CA 90211

Slamdance

Originally created in 1995 as an alternative to the nearby Sundance Festival, Slamdance takes place in Park City, Utah, at the same times as the Sundance Festival, making it possible for festival goers to attend screenings at both events.

The main feature competition is strictly for first-time directors with no distribution, but shorts and documentaries are also programmed. In 2003 about eighty films were screened, out of more than twenty-six hundred submissions. During the year the festival takes a selection of films "on the road" to other cities. It also sponsors monthly online short film competitions and a screenplay competition for writers who have never had a feature screenplay produced or distributed.

For more information contact:

Slamdance
5634 Melrose Avenue
Los Angeles, CA 90038
mail@slamdance.com
slamdance.com

San Francisco International Lesbian and Gay Film Festival

Started in 1976, this festival is the oldest and largest event of its kind, screening some of the world's finest lesbian, gay, bisexual, and transgender filmmaking. Events include competitions and special screenings. Frameline, a distribution company dedicated to lesbian and gay film and video, sponsors the festival.

For more information contact:

Frameline
145 Ninth Street, Suite 300
San Francisco, CA 94103-2636
info@frameline.org
frameline.org/festival

Ann Arbor Film Festival

This annual weeklong festival has been celebrating international experimental and independent films since 1963. Its goal is to promote film as art and create an alternative forum for not-so-mainstream films. Many awards are given under various categories such as Best Michigan Filmmaker and Amazing Audio Award.

For more information contact:

Ann Arbor Film Festival
P.O. Box 8232
Ann Arbor, MI 48107
info@aafilmfest.org
http://aafilmfest.org

Toronto International Film Festival

The TIFF started out in 1976 as a collection of films selected from other festivals. Since then it has undergone many changes and grown to become one of the most successful film festivals in the world, premiering very-high-profile films along with the works of lesser-known but worthwhile filmmakers, and in particular showcasing Canadian films.

Although films are awarded, the festival is not competitive. Some films featured in the festival throughout the years have been *Chariots of Fire*, *Boogie Nights*, and *Whale Rider*.

For more information contact:

Toronto International Film Festival
2 Carlton Street, Suite 1600
Toronto, ON M5B 1J3
Canada
tiffg@torfilmfest.ca

9

WOMEN AND MINORITIES

REALISTICALLY, WHAT CHANCES do women and minorities have today to succeed in the film industry? Over the years, the track record has been less than desirable.

"Women have had it tough in the technical areas," says Linda Rheinstein, vice president of The Post Group, a Los Angeles–based postproduction facility. "In sales and marketing, it's been a little easier."

Although men still heavily dominate the entertainment industry, women are forging their own paths. The lighter digital video cameras have made it easier for women to do the camera work and have direct control over the images. Many women are now in the business, allowing a network to form. Women's professional organizations are a positive resource that allow women to share experiences and develop strong group support systems.

Women in Film

Throughout much of the past, key positions in the film industry have been regarded as strictly part of an "old boys network," with few chances for women to be employed at higher levels. Fortunately that's changing, as barriers continue to fall.

Women in Film and its global committee, Women in Film International, are dedicated to breaking down those barriers. Created and founded in 1972 by Tichi Wilkerson Kassel, former publisher and editor-in-chief of *The Hollywood Reporter*, along with eight founding members, Women in Film was formed to aid women in all phases of the entertainment industry by increasing their visibility, helping them to network with their peers, and unifying professional women within the industry.

At the time, the number of women working in key positions in the industry—or in any position above the secretarial level—was minimal. There was an isolated woman writer, producer, or director, and there have always been women in costumes, makeup, and allied arts. But women in executive positions were rare.

Wilkerson Kassel herself was one of those women. Born in Los Angeles, a daughter of the Verdugo family—pioneer settlers of Mexico and California who came to North America in 1520 with explorer Hernando Cortez—Tichi (a diminutive of Beatriz) was raised in Mexico City and returned to Los Angeles as a teenager. When, as a young widow and mother of two, she inherited *The Hollywood Reporter*, she expanded the paper on a global level, turning it into one of the hundred most successful Latino companies in America. Never satisfied with the status quo, Tichi introduced two innovative programs that greatly increased the paper's international circulation and impact on the entertainment industry. One was the

Key Art Awards, which annually recognize outstanding artists in motion picture and television advertising/promotion. The other was *The Hollywood Reporter* Marketing Concept Awards, which offer recognition and cash prizes to those motion picture exhibitors who have originated the most imaginative and effective movie-marketing campaigns.

The beginnings of Women in Film were modest. Meetings were announced in the paper and held at *The Hollywood Reporter* offices. Wilkerson Kassel and Marcia Borie, one of the founding members and its first treasurer, would buy cheese and crackers and make a big pot of coffee, never knowing ahead of time how many people would attend. In fact, the first Christmas party, which was held at Tichi's home, found members and relatives making hors d'oeuvres to cut down on expenses.

Word of the organization spread rapidly, and before the end of its first year, Women in Film had more than 150 members. Long before the term "networking" became popular, the organization set up a job referral bureau, still in operation, to match qualified members with those able to offer work.

Today, benefits from Wilkerson Kassel's original concept are being enjoyed by more than two thousand women members in California and around the world.

Opportunities for Women Today

Though many more women currently are employed or freelancing in film than when Women in Film was founded, it still isn't easy for women to break into the industry. Consider the results of the Directors Guild of America's "Report on Women and Minority Hiring," published in June 2003. The report noted that in its study of the top forty prime-time drama and television series for the 2002–2003 season, women directed only 11 percent of the episodes, virtually the same amount as in the past two years.

How can individual women beat the odds? First of all everyone, regardless of gender, should be realistic. Film school students bewitched by the aura and glamour of motion pictures should realize the odds against success are high. For every graduate who walks into a studio in a good capacity, ninety-nine don't.

Second, be prepared for every contingency. Learn basic administrative skills, including working with a variety of office-based word processing programs. If the only way to get your foot in the door is as an administrative assistant, or gofer, take the job. You'll be working near a director or a producer and can learn by watching. More important, you'll be making contacts.

In addition, you should read the trade papers to learn who are the industry "movers and shakers"; have a good command of the English language; know films currently in the marketplace; and, if you are fortunate enough to make it, keep the faith by helping other women to succeed.

Wilkerson Kassel herself was honored when her star was placed on Hollywood's Walk of Fame. She and Borie have also coauthored *Hollywood Legends: The Golden Years of The Hollywood Reporter.*

Today, Women in Film boasts thousands of members, but its purpose is still the same: to provide networking and information for female professionals. Currently the group does that in a variety of ways: maintaining a speakers bureau; sponsoring screenings and panel discussions on relevant issues; providing financial assistance for education, research, and completion of film projects; and advocating within the industry for full participation by women.

To encourage the industry to hire and promote women, Women in Film sponsors the Crystal Awards and funds grants for studios and independent film companies that sponsor internships for women. Women in Film also educates its members directly by offering workshops, lectures, and discussions on directing, producing, contract negotiation, writing, production development, acting, and technical crafts.

The original Women in Film chapter is the one based in Los Angeles, but now there are chapters all over the world, connected to each other through Women in Film and Television International.

For more information contact:

Women in Film, Los Angeles
8857 Olympic Boulevard, Suite 201
Beverly Hills, CA 90211
(310) 657-5144, ext.10
wiforg.com

New York Women in Film and Television
6 East Thirty-Ninth Street, 12th Floor
New York, NY 10016
nywift.org

The Association for Women in Communications, Inc.

With networking, seminars, workshops, and conventions, the Association for Women in Communications, Inc. (AWC) is an association those interested in a career in the film industry will find well worth joining.

Although its members work in other fields besides film, the AWC is an association dedicated to promoting the advancement of women. Founded in 1909 as Theta Sigma Phi at the University of Washington in Seattle, the AWC unites women and men from all fields of communications. Professional members come from advertising, communications, education, film, magazines, newspapers, photojournalism, public relations, publishing, radio, technical writing, and television. The AWC has more than seven thousand professional, student, and independent members.

At its professional conference, held annually, the AWC offers seminars and workshops designed to help communicators improve professional skills and knowledge and advance their careers. The AWC's regional chapters also host annual professional development conferences. Both professional and student chapters offer frequent workshops and seminars.

AWC members on the local, regional, and national levels have access to job referrals (including a national job hotline), special programs, internships, and other career aids and materials. The group presents the Vanguard Awards to companies that actively hire and promote women to positions of equality.

For more information contact:

The Association for Women in Communications, Inc.
780 Ritchie Highway, Suite 28-S
Severna Park, MD 21146
womcom.org

A Success Story

Postproduction executive Linda Carol Rheinstein says she was "born into the business" as the daughter of a father who owned a production company and a mother who'd been a dancer-choreographer on "Your Show of Shows" at NBC. At thirteen, Rheinstein's first paying job was as a production assistant for CBS Sports on the "Acapulco Aquacade," and in 1972 she worked for

NBC News as a production assistant at the Republican National Convention.

By the time she was nineteen, she'd been a runner (gofer), a crew coordinator, a production assistant, an associate producer in audio mixing, a technical director, and a camera-chyron operator, using technical equipment that generates alphanumeric characters electronically—all this for her father's production company.

Her father wanted her to go on to school; Rheinstein didn't. "I took my college money and, at age nineteen, started my own company. Basically, I was Autographics. I did maintenance, I operated the chyron, I was management—have chyron, will travel!"

Computer graphics became her field. In 1983, when she bought an Aurora 100 (another graphics machine), The Post Group, a Los Angeles postproduction company, asked her to join its staff and develop its graphics department.

Under her leadership, Autographics and The Post Group, along with video designer/artist Tony Redhead, started Electric Paint—the first U.S. company to use the new technology that made it possible to create digital transparencies for print. Electric Paint does original art for movie posters, record album covers, billboards, and the printed page.

Rheinstein and The Post Group also worked with Pacific Title and Art to develop a theatrical-quality tape-to-film process that allows graphics and special effects to be used in film work.

The Post Group became one of the largest, most successful graphics facilities in the world. The company, which opened its graphics center in 1986, moved to its digital center in 1990, combining graphics, editing, and telecine in one location.

Rheinstein became vice president of The Post Group Enterprises and was responsible for marketing, advertising, and promotion for the company and its graphics center.

Rheinstein admits success as a woman has been easier for her because she started her own companies. She considers herself a pioneering woman in the business. "What has allowed me to succeed," she says, "is that I know my job, and I am good."

Her advice to women: "Listen. Learn from others. Pick a good role model, and don't carry a chip on your shoulder. Concentrate on your goals."

She emphasizes that anyone wanting to succeed today must keep up with technology. If it's difficult for students to get hands-on experience, she strongly suggests they read the trade magazines. "Learn to spot opportunities," she advises. "They exist. Or make your own!"

Opportunities for Minorities

Over the years, minorities, too, have been gaining greater presence in the film and television industry as their movies and other productions receive acclaim and organizations are formed to help advance their careers.

Asian-American Cinema and Television

Asian-Americans have been one of the most underrepresented groups in the film and television industry. Although they still are experiencing difficulty breaking into the business, there are some encouraging signs of change on both the big and the small screens.

Over the last few years, Asian and Asian-American actors have been gaining a presence on the screen: Chow Yun-Fat, Jet Li, Jackie Chan, Margaret Cho, Lucy Liu. Even better, Asian-American directors have gained success behind the camera. M. Night Shyamalan, Ang Lee, and Mira Nair are some of the more famous examples.

Asian-American-theme films may now be considered marketable, as suggested by MTV's acquisition of *Better Luck Tomorrow*. But this does not mean Asian-Americans are represented proportionately in American film and television.

To see new works by Asian-American filmmakers, you can attend one of the several Asian-American film festivals held annually throughout the country. The San Francisco International Asian-American Film and Video Festival, founded in 1982, is one of the largest and most influential showcases for new Asian-American talent. The National Asian-American Telecommunications Association (NAATA) sponsors the festival. It receives attention from industry professionals, local media, and the industry press.

For information on the festival, or to learn more about how the NAATA serves as a resource for information, funding, and exhibition of film projects, contact the NAATA at:

National Asian-American Telecommunications Association
145 Ninth Street, Suite 350
San Francisco, CA 94103
naata@naatanet.org
naata.org

Opportunities for African-Americans

Though you may not be familiar with African-American films from before Spike Lee, The American Film Institute (AFI) has, in its collection at the Library of Congress, an extensive selection of all-black-cast films. Most were released between the early 1920s and the late 1940s. A highly controversial film, *The Birth of a Race*, was produced in 1918 as a black response to the racism of D. W. Griffith's *The Birth of a Nation*, released in 1915. Some are early experimental talking pictures produced by Lee DeForest.

The key all-black-cast filmmaker in those early years was Oscar Micheaux, who made more than thirty features between 1918 and 1948. A number of his films are included in the AFI collection.

But African-Americans seeking employment in mainstream film, especially since the Depression, have found it difficult. In the beginning, African-Americans in mainstream film were almost always portrayed in stereotyped roles. Butterfly McQueen's, "Lordy, Miss Scarlet, I don't know nothin' 'bout birthin' babies!" from *Gone With the Wind* is reminiscent of typical dialogue. Later, Sidney Poitier, Harry Belafonte, Dorothy Dandridge, Diahann Carroll, and Diana Ross came to prominence but have rarely had the opportunities available to white talent.

In the late 1960s and early 1970s, African-Americans began to graduate from film schools like UCLA, NYU, and Yale. They found breaking into film production was difficult. Yet they pursued their goals.

Black filmmaker Spike Lee's feature *School Daze*, panned by most white newspaper critics, grossed fifteen million dollars to become one of Columbia's most profitable theatrical releases of 1988. The movie magazine *Premiere* described Lee as "the first black director ever bankrolled by Hollywood who's been given complete control." In an in-depth interview, he told *Premiere*: "I'm an independent filmmaker, but I don't scrape around for money. I go directly to Hollywood for my financing. It doesn't really mess with my creativity, because I have the final cut and the control over the film that I would have had if I'd raised the money all by myself. Even if I had, I'd still have to go to Hollywood for distribution anyway—there's just no way I'm going to reach the people I want to reach carrying a film can under my arm and going from theater to theater across the country."

Lee, says *Premiere*, tries to get African-Americans on his crews and into the unions. "Wherever possible, he used black talent to shoot, score, and coproduce his films." Yet in *Do the Right Thing* (1989), a controversial film about prejudice and ethnic violence in Brooklyn's Bedford-Stuyvesant neighborhood, Lee used white actors when the story required, "because the film involves white people."

Things improved slowly in the 1990s. Statistics from the Screen Actors Guild (SAG) indicate that in 2002 black actors and actresses received 14.4 percent of all roles given to SAG actors, down from 14.8 percent in 2000, with a larger share of roles in TV than theatrical films. This leaves considerable room for improvement, especially given the fact that African-Americans comprise almost a quarter of the movie-going public. Certainly there is a large pool of talent to draw from—Laurence Fishburne, Angela Bassett, Samuel L. Jackson, and Will Smith, to mention just a few.

Behind the camera, African-Americans are also making some strides. The number of black producers and directors is slowly increasing, thanks in part to the rise of independent filmmaking, and the African-American experience is being brought to the big screen in powerful documentaries like John Singleton's *Rosewood* and Spike Lee's *Four Little Girls*.

There are some noteworthy success stories: There is Robert L. Johnson's rise from small-town poverty in Illinois to the management of the cable giant Black Entertainment Television. And few actresses—of any ethnicity—can match Whoopi Goldberg or Oprah Winfrey's accomplishments and power in the industry. These role models are paving the way for greater participation by blacks in all aspects of the film and television industry.

In 2002, for the first time, two African-American actors, Halle Berry and Denzel Washington, won Academy Awards. This was considered a big step for African-Americans in Hollywood, but there are more categories still to be won.

Opportunities for Latinos

Like other minorities, Latino filmmakers are an underrepresented but growing voice in the film industry. It has been more than two decades since filmmaker Efrain Gutierrez created the first Chicano feature film, the 1976 hit *Please Don't Bury Me Alive*. Since that time other outstanding works by Latino filmmakers have broken through the industry barriers to impress the Hollywood community. The Robert Rodriquez film *El Mariachi*, produced for just $7,000, is a legend in independent film history. More recently, filmmakers like Alfonso Cuarón, Guillermo del Toro, and Patricia Cardoso have been making films that reflect their culture and do well at the box office.

One of the most respected professionals in film today is Latino screenwriter-director Gregory Nava, who created the Oscar-nominated *El Norte* in 1983. A more recent film by Nava is *My Family*, which portrays the struggles of a Latino family in Los Angeles. When interviewed about *My Family* in the *Los Angeles Times*, Nava said: "It's been my dream for many years to make a film about a Latino family. We aren't just individuals; we are each a product of our families. *Familia* is the very center of Latino culture. I don't feel the media has really seen that. It is the strongest thing about us and the most universal."

At the time, Nava hoped the film would appeal to a wide audience while still delivering a special message to Latinos: "It speaks to the universality of human experience. It's about family—over and above the Latino family. Those relationships are universal. But to Latinos, I want to convey a sense of the depth and beauty of our culture." Since then Nava has worked on several high-profile projects about Latinos, including *Selena* and the award-winning film *Frida*.

In the television world, Latinos have not gained much presence, except on the highly successful networks targeting Latinos. The growing power of Latinos as consumers is just beginning to have an effect on their representation in mainstream media.

If you would like to see new films by Latinos, check out one of the many Latino/Hispanic film festivals. The New York International Latino Film Festival, for example, exists to showcase films that offer a comprehensive view of the Latino experience and to assist emerging Latino filmmakers in presenting their work to a broader audience. For more information contact:

New York International Latino Film Festival
445 West Forty-Ninth Street
New York, NY 10019
info@nylatinofilm.com
nylatinofilm.com

Change Is Slow

Despite the increased visibility of minorities in recent years, Asians, blacks, and Latinos still are not working as regularly in the industry as anyone would like. According to the Directors Guild of America's 2003 hiring report for the top forty prime-time shows, minorities as a whole accounted for only 8 percent of episodes directed.

In response to the lack of minority directors, the DGA held its first diversity summit in 1997, bringing top industry executives and directors together to discuss the problems facing women and ethnic minority directors and assistant directors. The DGA Diversity Award was created to honor producers and employers who demonstrate a commitment to hiring women and minorities as directors.

The DGA's African-American, Asian, Latino, and women's committees also make concerted efforts to introduce directors to producers, studio representatives, and other employers. The ceiling is hard to break through but, slowly, working minority directors and other production personnel are gaining in numbers as well as visibility.

10

FILM IN CANADA

THE HISTORY OF Canadian filmmaking is one of overcoming obstacles and struggling to compete for its audience with American movies. Although great films have been made, the real challenge has been for Canada to build a national film cultural identity.

Today the film and television industry in Canada is worth about $2 billion annually. Of that amount, nearly half, or $700 million, is from outside productions, mostly from North America. Foreign film production inside Canada is growing, even outside the major urban centers such as Toronto and Vancouver. In the mid-1990s, nearly three dozen films were shot in British Columbia, and Nova Scotia has become the most developed film industry locale in the Maritime provinces.

In the world of television, the Canadian Broadcasting Corporation (CBC) noticed Canadians' interest in American TV in 1945 and set about building a Canadian service, over which it had a monopoly until 1962. When private stations started appearing, the government created Canadian content quotas to ensure that original Canadian programs would continue to be produced.

The last few years have been a period of growth for the Canadian production industry. In part this is due to the aggressiveness of various government-sponsored organizations that vigorously solicit motion picture companies from all over the world, pointing out the advantages of filming in Canada and offering financial incentives. Vancouver has become a popular location for American television productions, such as "X-Files" and "24."

Also in recent years, a number of Canadian films, such as *The Red Violin*, *Atanarjuat*, and *Ararat*, have received acclaim from overseas, building the international market for Canadian-made movies.

Filming in British Columbia

The history of filming in British Columbia is longer than most people think. The industry began in 1913 and saw the first influx of filmmakers and stars from Hollywood in 1930. The area's first global television hit was "The Littlest Hobo," which was shot from 1963 to 1965 and syndicated around the world. In 2002, British Columbia hosted nearly two hundred productions, creating a billion-dollar film industry in one province alone. It is the third-largest film production center in North America, following New York and Los Angeles.

In addition to film production, it should be noted that British Columbia hosts a well-respected film school. Vancouver Film School (VFS) offers accelerated programs that focus exclusively on the production of the moving image. Its graduates have had success working in film, television, and new media production throughout North America and the world.

VFS offers portfolio production programs in the following areas:

- Film
- 2-D animation
- 3-D computer animation
- Acting for film and television
- Interactive media
- Writing for film and television
- Makeup
- Sound design

For information contact the school at:

Vancouver Film School
198 West Hastings Street, Suite 200
Vancouver, BC V6B 1H2
Canada
vfs.com

Contact the following film resources for more information on the film industry in British Columbia:

British Columbia Film
2225 West Broadway
Vancouver, BC V6K 2E4
Canada
bcfilm.bc.ca

British Columbia Film Commission
#201-865 Hornby Street
Vancouver, BC V62 2G3
Canada
bcfilmcommission.com

National Film Board of Canada

Any discussion of Canadian film should include the National Film Board of Canada (NFB), founded more than sixty years ago "to initiate and promote the production and distribution of films in the national interests, and in particular . . . to interpret Canada to Canadians and to other countries."

With more than nine thousand titles in its collection, the NFB is a public agency that produces and distributes films and considers itself a cultural organization as well as a center for filmmaking and video technology. NFB productions have won nine Oscars, and the organization itself won an honorary Oscar "in recognition of its dedicated commitment to originate artistic, creative, and technological activity and excellence in every area of filmmaking."

For more information about the board contact:

National Film Board of Canada
P.O. Box 6100
Station Centre-ville
Montreal, QC H3C 3H5
Canada
nfb.ca/e

Canadian Film Centre

The Canadian Film Centre's mission is "to advance the artistic and technical skills of writers, directors, and producers in support of a dynamic industry, and to increase the awareness and appreciation of Canadian film and television." It provides training for directors, writers, producers, and new media professionals. A key component of the center is the Feature Film Project, which offers financing to Canadian independent filmmakers.

For more information you can contact the centre at:

Canadian Film Centre
Windfields
2489 Bayview Avenue
Toronto, ON M2L 1A8
Canada
cdnfilmcentre.com

Canadian Film Institute

The Canadian Film Institute is the oldest film institution in Canada. Its mission is to promote the production and study of film and video for cultural and educational purposes, through film programming, distribution, and publication of books on Canadian filmmaking.

For more information about its programs contact:

Canadian Film Institute
2 Daly Avenue
Ottawa, ON K1N 6E2
Canada
cfi-icf.ca

Canadian Film and Television Production Association

The CFTPA's mission is to promote and stimulate the Canadian production industry, supporting independent producers with training, networking opportunities, and assistance negotiating labor agreements. CFTPA offices are located in Ottawa, Toronto, and Vancouver. It also created *GUIDE*, a widely used industry directory.

CFTPA Ottawa
151 Slater Street, Suite 605
Ottawa, ON K1P 5H3
Canada
cftpa.ca

Women in Film and Television—Toronto

Women in Film and Television—Toronto is an internationally affil-
iated professional organization of more than seven hundred members whose mission is to "enhance the opportunities for women in
the industry nationally and internationally, to provide leadership
and to celebrate the accomplishments of women in film and television." It achieves this goal by offering seminars, training courses,
and workshops as well as screenings and a regular series on networking. The organization maintains a presence at the influential
Toronto Film Festival and publishes the quarterly newsletter *Changing Focus*.

For information on the group contact:

Women in Film and Television—Toronto
2300 Yonge Street, Suite 405
P.O. Box 2386
Toronto, ON M4P 1E4
Canada
wift.com

11

RÉSUMÉS AND COVER LETTERS

YOUR RÉSUMÉ IS a piece of paper (or an electronic document) that serves to introduce you to the people who will eventually hire you. To write a thoughtful résumé, you must thoroughly assess your personality, your accomplishments, and the skills you have acquired. The act of composing and submitting a résumé also requires you to carefully consider the company or individual in the film and television industry who might hire you. What is he or she looking for, and how can you meet the company's needs?

Writing the résumé is just one step in what can be a daunting job-search process, but it is an important element in the chain of events that will lead you to your new position. While you are probably a talented, bright, and charming person, your résumé may not reflect these qualities. A poorly written résumé can get you nowhere; a well-written résumé can land you an interview and potentially a job. A good résumé can even lead the interviewer to ask you questions that will allow you to talk about your strengths and highlight the skills you can bring to a job in film and television. Even a person with very little experience can find a good job if he or she is assisted by a thoughtful and polished résumé.

Lengthy, typewritten résumés are a thing of the past. Today employers in film and television do not have the time or the patience for verbose documents; they look for tightly composed, straightforward, action-based résumés. Although a one-page résumé is the norm, a two-page résumé may be warranted if you have had extensive film or television experience or have changed careers and truly need the space to properly position yourself. If, after careful editing, you still need more than one page to present yourself, it's acceptable to use a second page. A crowded résumé that's hard to read would be the worst of your choices.

Distilling your work experience, education, and interests into such a small space requires preparation and thought. This chapters takes you through a step-by-step process of crafting an effective résumé that will stand out in today's competitive marketplace.

The Elements of an Effective Résumé

An effective résumé is composed of information that employers are most interested in knowing about a prospective job applicant. This information is conveyed by a few essential elements. The following is a list of elements that are found in most résumés—some essential, some optional. Later in this chapter, we will further examine the role of each of these elements in the makeup of your résumé.

- Heading
- Objective and/or keyword section
- Work experience
- Education
- Honors

- Activities
- Professional memberships
- References

The first step in preparing your résumé is to gather information about yourself and your past accomplishments that may be relevant in the industry. Later you will refine this information, rewrite it using effective language, and organize it into an attractive layout. But first let's take a look at each of these important elements individually so you can judge their appropriateness for your résumé.

Heading

Although the heading may seem to be the simplest section of your résumé, be careful not to take it lightly. It is the first section a producer, director, or other employer will see, and it contains the information she or he will need to contact you. At the very least, the heading must contain your name, your home address, and, of course, a phone number where you can be reached easily.

In today's high-tech world, many of us have multiple ways that we can be contacted. You may list your e-mail address if you are reasonably sure the employer makes use of this form of communication. Keep in mind, however, that others may have access to your e-mail messages if you send them from an account provided by your current company. If this is a concern, do not list your work e-mail address on your résumé. If you are able to take calls at your current place of business, you should include your work number, because most employers will attempt to contact you during typical business hours.

If you have voice mail or a reliable answering machine at home or at work, list its number in the heading and make sure your greeting is professional and clear. Always include at least one phone number in your heading, even if it is a temporary number, where a prospective employer can leave a message.

You might have a dozen different ways to be contacted, but you do not need to list all of them. Confine your numbers or addresses to those that are the easiest for the prospective employer to use and the simplest for you to retrieve.

Objective

When seeking a specific career path, it is important to list a job or career objective on your résumé. This statement helps employers know the direction you see yourself taking, so they can determine whether your goals are in line with theirs. Normally, an objective is one to two sentences long. Its contents will vary depending on what your goals in the industry are and your personality. The objective can be specific or general, but it should always be to the point.

If you are planning to use this résumé online, or you suspect your potential employer is likely to scan your résumé, you will want to include a "keyword" in the objective. This allows a prospective employer, searching hundreds of résumés for a specific skill or position objective, to locate the keyword and find your résumé. In essence, a keyword is what's "hot" in your particular field at a given time. It's a buzzword, a shorthand way of getting a particular message across at a glance.

There are many résumé and job-search sites online. Like most things in the online world, they vary a great deal in quality. Use your discretion. If you plan to apply for jobs online or advertise your availability this way, you will want to design a résumé that is easily scanned. This type of résumé uses a format that can be scanned into a computer and added to a database. Scanning allows a prospective employer to use keywords to quickly review each applicant's experience and skills, and (in the event that there are many candidates for the job) to keep your résumé for future reference.

Many people find it worthwhile to create two or more versions of their basic résumé. You may want an intricately designed résumé on high-quality paper to mail or hand out and a résumé that is designed to be scanned into a computer and saved on a database or an online job site. You can even create a résumé in ASCII text to e-mail to prospective employers.

Although it is usually a good idea to include an objective, in some cases this element is not necessary. As already mentioned, the goal of the objective statement is to provide the employer with an idea of where you see yourself going in the field. However, if you are uncertain of the exact nature of the job you seek, including an objective that is too specific could result in your not being considered for a host of perfectly acceptable positions. If you decide not to use an objective heading in your résumé, you should definitely incorporate the information that would be conveyed in the objective into your cover letter.

Work Experience

Your work experience in film and television is arguably the most important element of them all. Unless you are a recent graduate or have little or no relevant work experience, your current and former positions will provide the central focus of the résumé. You will want this section to be as complete and carefully constructed as possible. By thoroughly examining your work experience, you can get to the heart of your accomplishments and present them in a way that demonstrates and highlights your qualifications.

If you are just entering the workforce, your résumé will probably focus on your education, but you should also include information on your extracurricular, internship, or volunteer experiences.

Although you will have less information about work experience than a person who has held multiple positions or is advanced in his or her career, the amount of information is not what is most important in this section. How the information is presented and what it says about you as a worker and a person is what really counts.

As you create this section of your résumé, remember the need for accuracy. Include all the necessary information about each of your jobs, including your job title, dates of employment, name of your employer, city, state, responsibilities, special projects you handled, and accomplishments. Be sure to list only accomplishments for which you were directly responsible. Don't be alarmed if you haven't participated in or worked on special projects, because this section may not be relevant to certain jobs.

The most common way to list your work experience is in reverse chronological order. In other words, start with your most recent job and work your way backward. This way, your prospective employer sees your current (and often most important) position before considering your past employment. Your most recent position, if it's the most important in terms of responsibilities and relevance to the job for which you are applying, should also be the one that includes the most information as compared to your previous positions.

Even if the work itself seems unrelated to your proposed career path, you should list any job or experience that will help "sell" your talents. If you won student film competitions or were promoted or given greater responsibilities or commendations, be sure to mention the fact.

Education

Education is usually the second most important element of a résumé. Highlight your accomplishments in school as much as you did those accomplishments at work. Include in this section all the degrees or certificates you have received; your major or area of concentration, all of the honors you earned, and any relevant activities you participated in, organized, or chaired.

List your most recent schooling first. If you have completed a large number of credit hours in a subject that may be relevant to the position you are seeking, but did not obtain a degree, you may wish to list the hours or classes you completed. If you are currently in school, list the degree, certificate, or license you expect to obtain and the projected date of completion.

Honors

If you include an honors section in your résumé, you should highlight any awards, honors, or memberships in honorary societies that you have received. Often the honors are academic in nature, but this section also may be used for special achievements in film and video or other school activities. Always include the name of the organization awarding the honor and the date(s) received.

Activities

Perhaps you have been active in different organizations or clubs; often an employer will look at such involvement as evidence of initiative, dedication, and good social skills. Examples of your ability to take a leading role in a group should be included on a résumé, if you can provide them. The activities section of your résumé should present neighborhood and community activities, volunteer positions, and so forth.

Professional Memberships

Another potential element in your résumé is a section that lists professional memberships. Use this section to describe your involvement in professional associations, unions, and similar organizations in the film and television industry. It is to your advantage to list any professional memberships that pertain to the job you are seeking. Include the dates of your involvement and whether you took part in any special activities or held any offices within the organization.

References

References are not usually given on the résumé itself, but a prospective employer needs to know that you have references who may be contacted if necessary. All you need to include is a single sentence at the end of the résumé: "References are available upon request," or even simply, "References available." Have a reference list ready—your interviewer may ask to see it. Contact each person on the list ahead of time to see whether it is all right for you to use him or her as a reference. This way, the person has a chance to think about what to say before the call occurs.

Writing Your Résumé

Résumé writing is unlike any other form of writing. Although your seventh-grade composition teacher would not approve, the rules of punctuation and sentence building are often completely ignored. Instead, you should try for a functional, direct writing style that focuses on the use of verbs and other words that imply action on your part. Writing with action words and strong verbs characterizes you to potential employers as an energetic, active person, someone who completes tasks and achieves results from his or her work. Résumés that do not make use of action words can sound passive and stale. These résumés are not effective and do not get the attention of any employer, no matter how qualified the applicant.

Choose words that display your strengths and demonstrate your initiative.

One helpful way to construct the work experience section is to make use of your actual job descriptions—the written duties and expectations your employers had for a person in your current or former position. Job descriptions are rarely written in proper résumé language, so you will have to rework them, but they do include much of the information necessary to create this section of your résumé. If you have access to job descriptions for your former positions, you can use the details to construct an action-oriented paragraph. Often, your human resources department can provide a job description for your current position.

Assembly

The order of the elements in a résumé makes a difference in its overall effect. Clearly you would not want to bury your name and address somewhere in the middle of the résumé. Nor would you want to lead with a less important section, such as special skills. Put the elements in an order that stresses your most important accomplishments and the things that will be most appealing to your potential employer. For example, if you are new to the workforce, you will want the reviewer to read about your education and film and video skills before any part-time jobs you may have held for short durations. On the other hand, if you have been gainfully employed for several years and currently hold an important position in your company, you should list your work accomplishments ahead of your educational information, which has become less pertinent with time.

Always use information that will put you in a favorable light—unless it's absolutely essential, avoid anything that will prompt the interviewer to ask questions about your weaknesses or something else that could be unflattering. Make sure your information is accurate and truthful. If your honors are impressive, include them in the résumé. If your activities in school demonstrate talents that are necessary for the job you are seeking, allow space for a section on activities. If you are applying for a position that requires editing skills, for example, you may want to include a tape or DVD that demonstrate your talents in this area. If you are answering an advertisement for a job that requires certain physical traits, a photo of yourself might be appropriate. However, a person applying for a job as a gaffer would not include a photo as part of his or her résumé. Each résumé is unique, just as each person is unique.

Types of Résumés

So far we have focused on the most common type of résumé—the reverse chronological résumé—in which your most recent job is listed first. This is the type of résumé usually preferred by those who have to read a large number of résumés, and it is by far the most popular and widely circulated. However, this style of presentation may not be the most effective way to highlight your skills and accomplishments.

For example, if you are reentering the workforce after many years or are trying to change career fields, the functional résumé may work best. This type of résumé puts the focus on your achievements instead of the sequence of your work history. In the functional résumé, your experience is presented through your general accomplishments and the skills you have developed in your working life.

The main difference lies in how you organize the information. Essentially, the work experience section is divided in two, with your job duties and accomplishments constituting one section and your employers' names, cities, and states; your positions; and the dates employed making up the other. Place the first section near the top of your résumé, just below your job objective (if used), and call it Accomplishments or Achievements. The second section, containing the bare essentials of your work history, should come after the accomplishments section and can be called Employment History, since it is a chronological overview of your former jobs.

The other sections of your résumé remain the same. The work experience section is the only one affected in the functional format. By placing the section that focuses on your achievements at the beginning, you draw attention to these achievements. This puts less emphasis on whom you worked for and when, and more on what you did and what you are capable of doing.

If you are changing careers, the emphasis on skills and achievements is important. The identities of previous employers (who aren't part of your new career field) need to be downplayed. A functional résumé can help accomplish this task. If you are reentering the workforce after a long absence, a functional résumé is the obvious choice. If you lack full-time work experience, you will need to draw attention away from this fact and put the focus on your skills and abilities. You may need to highlight your extracurricular activities and part-time work in film and video. Education may also play a more important role in your résumé.

The type of résumé that is right for you will depend on your personal circumstances. It may be helpful to create both types and then compare them. Which one presents you in the best light?

Special Tips for Electronic Résumés

There are many details to consider in writing a résumé that will be posted or transmitted on the Internet; here are some brief, general guidelines to follow if you expect your résumé to be scanned into a computer.

- Use standard fonts in which none of the letters touch.
- Keep in mind that underlining, italics, and fancy scripts may not scan well.
- Use boldface and capitalization to set off elements. Again, make sure letters don't touch. Leave at least a quarter inch between lines of type.
- Keep information and elements at the left margin. Centering, columns, and even indenting may change when the résumé is optically scanned.
- Do not use any lines, boxes, or graphics.
- Place the most important information at the top of the first page. If you use two pages, put "Page 1 of 2" at the bottom of the first page and put your name and "Page 2 of 2" at the top of the second page.
- List each telephone number on its own line in the header.
- Use multiple keywords or synonyms for what you do to make sure your qualifications will be picked up if a prospective employer is searching for them. Use nouns that are keywords for your profession.
- Be descriptive in your titles. For example, don't just use "assistant"; use "best boy."
- Make sure the contrast between print and paper is good. Use a high-quality laser printer and white or very light colored 8½-by-11-inch paper.
- Mail a high-quality laser print or an excellent photocopy. Do not fold or use staples, as this might interfere with scanning. You may, however, use paper clips.

In addition to creating a résumé that works well for scanning, you may want to have a résumé that can be e-mailed to reviewers.

Because you may not know what word processing application the recipient uses, the best format to use is ASCII text. (ASCII stands for American Standard Code for Information Exchange.) It allows people with very different software platforms to exchange and understand information. (E-mail operates on this principle.) ASCII is a simple, text-only language, which means you can include only simple text. There can be no use of boldface, italics, or even paragraph indentations.

To create an ASCII résumé, just use your normal word processing program; when finished, save it as a "text only" document. You will find this option under the "save" or "save as" command. Here is a list of things to avoid when crafting your electronic résumé:

- Tabs. Use your space bar; tabs will not work.
- Any special characters. These include, for example, mathematical symbols.
- Word wrap. Use hard returns (the return key) to make line breaks.
- Centering or other formatting. Align everything at the left margin.
- Bold or italic fonts. Everything will be converted to plain text when you save the file as a "text only" document.

Check carefully for any mistakes before you save the document as a text file. Spell-check and proofread it several times; then ask someone with a keen eye to go over it again for you. Remember: the key is to keep it simple. Any attempt to make this résumé pretty or decorative may result in a résumé that is confusing and hard to read. After you have saved the document, you can cut and paste it into an e-mail or onto a website.

Layout

A great deal of care—and much more formatting—is necessary to achieve an attractive layout for your paper résumé. There is no single appropriate layout that applies to every résumé, but there are a few basic rules to follow in putting your résumé on paper:

- Leave a comfortable margin on the sides, top, and bottom of the page (usually one to one and a half inches).
- Use appropriate spacing between the sections (two- or three-line spaces are usually adequate).
- Be consistent in the type of headings you use for different sections of your résumé. For example, if you capitalize the heading EMPLOYMENT HISTORY, don't use initial capitals and underlining for a section of equal importance, such as Education.
- Do not use more than one font in your résumé. Stay consistent by choosing a font that is fairly standard and easy to read, and don't change it for different sections. Beware of the tendency to try to make your résumé original by choosing fancy type styles; your résumé may end up looking unprofessional instead of creative. Unless you are very creative and artistic, you should almost always stick with tried-and-true type styles like Times New Roman and Palatino, which are often used in business writing. In the area of résumé styles, conservative is usually the best way to go.
- Always try to fit your résumé on one page. If you are having trouble with this, you may be trying to say too much. Edit out any repetitive or unnecessary information, and shorten descriptions of earlier jobs where possible. Ask a friend you trust for feedback on what seems unnecessary or unim-

portant. For example, you may have included too many optional sections. Today, with the prevalence of the personal computer as a tool, there is no excuse for a poorly laid out résumé. Experiment with variations until you are pleased with the result.

Remember that a résumé is not an autobiography. Too much information will only get in the way. The more compact your résumé, the easier it will be to review. If a person who is swamped with résumés looks at yours, catches the main points, and then calls you for an interview to fill in some of the details, your résumé has already accomplished its task. A clear and concise résumé makes for a happy reader and a good impression.

There are times when, despite extensive editing, the résumé simply cannot fit on one page. In this case, the résumé should be laid out on two pages in such a way that neither clarity nor appearance is compromised. Each page of a two-page résumé should be marked clearly: the first should indicate "Page 1 of 2," and the second should include your name and the page number, for example, "Julia Ramirez—Page 2 of 2." The pages should then be stapled together. You may use a smaller font (in the same font as the body of your résumé) for the page numbers. Place them at the bottom of page one and the top of page two. Again, spend the time now to experiment with the layout until you find one that looks good to you.

Always show your final layout to other people and ask them what they like or dislike about it and what impresses them most when they read your résumé. Make sure that their responses are the same as what you want to elicit from your prospective employer. If they aren't the same, you should continue to make changes until the necessary information is emphasized.

Proofreading

After you have finished typing the master copy of your résumé and before you have it copied or printed, thoroughly check it for typing and spelling errors. Do not place all your trust in your computer's spell-check function. Use an old editing trick and read the whole résumé backward—start at the end and read it right to left and bottom to top. This can help you see the small errors or inconsistencies that are easy to overlook. Take time to do it right because a single error on a document this important can cause the reader to judge your attention to detail in a harsh light.

Have several people look at the finished résumé just in case you've missed an error. Don't try to take a shortcut; not having an unbiased set of eyes examine your résumé now could mean embarrassment later. Even experienced editors can easily overlook their own errors. Be thorough and conscientious with your proofreading so your first impression is a perfect one.

Cover Letters

Once your résumé has been assembled, laid out, and printed to your satisfaction, the final step before distribution is to write your cover letter. Though there may be instances where you deliver your résumé in person, you will usually send it through the mail or online. Résumés sent through the mail always need an accompanying letter that briefly introduces you and your résumé. The purpose of the cover letter is to get a potential employer to read your résumé, just as the purpose of the résumé is to get that same potential employer to call you for an interview.

Like your résumé, your cover letter should be clean, neat, and direct. A cover letter usually includes the following information:

1. Your name and address (unless it already appears on your personal letterhead) and your phone number(s); see item 7.
2. The date.
3. The name and address of the person and company to whom you are sending your résumé.
4. The salutation ("Dear Mr." or "Dear Ms." followed by the person's last name, or "To Whom It May Concern" if you are answering a blind ad).
5. An opening paragraph explaining why you are writing (for example, in response to an ad, as a follow-up to a previous meeting, at the suggestion of someone you both know) and indicating that you are interested in whatever job is being offered.
6. One or more paragraphs that tell why you want to work for the company and what qualifications and experiences you can bring to the position. This is a good place to mention some detail about that particular company that makes you want to work for it; this shows that you have done some research before applying.
7. A final paragraph that closes the letter and invites the reviewer to contact you for an interview. This can be a good place to tell the potential employer which method would be best to use when contacting you. Be sure to give the correct phone number and a good time to reach you, if that is important. You may mention here that your references are available upon request.
8. The closing ("Sincerely" or "Yours truly") followed by your signature in a dark ink, with your name typed under it.

Your cover letter should include all of this information and be no longer than one page in length. The language used should be polite, businesslike, and to the point. Don't attempt to tell your life story in the cover letter; a long and cluttered letter will serve only to annoy the reader. Remember that you need to mention only a few of your accomplishments and skills in the cover letter. The rest of your information is available in your résumé. If your cover letter is a success, your résumé will be read and all pertinent information reviewed by your prospective employer.

Producing the Cover Letter

Cover letters should always be individualized because they are always written to specific individuals and companies. Never use a form letter for your cover letter or copy it as you would a résumé. Each cover letter should be unique and as personal and lively as possible. (Of course, once you have written and rewritten your first cover letter until you are satisfied with it, you can certainly use similar wording in subsequent letters. You may want to save a template on your computer for future reference.) Keep a hard copy of each cover letter so you know exactly what you wrote in each one.

After you have written your cover letter, proofread it as thoroughly as you did your résumé. Again, spelling or punctuation errors are a sure sign of carelessness, and you don't want that to be a part of your first impression on a prospective employer. This is no time to trust your spell-check function. Even after going through a spelling and grammar check, your cover letter should be carefully proofread by at least one other person.

Print the cover letter on the same quality bond paper you used for your résumé. Remember to sign it, using a good, dark-ink pen. Handle the letter and résumé carefully to avoid smudging or wrinkling, and mail them together in an appropriately sized envelope.

Many stores sell matching envelopes to coordinate with your choice of bond paper.

Keep an accurate record of all résumés you send out and the results of each mailing. This record can be kept on your computer, in a calendar or notebook, or on file cards. Knowing when a résumé is likely to have been received will keep you on track as you make follow-up phone calls.

About a week after mailing résumés and cover letters to potential employers, contact them by telephone. Confirm that your résumé arrived and ask whether an interview might be possible. Be sure to record the name of the person you spoke with and any other information you gleaned from the conversation. It is wise to treat the person answering the phone with a great deal of respect; sometimes the assistant or receptionist has the ear of the person doing the hiring.

Appendix A

Periodicals

There are a number of periodicals connected with the film and video industry. Most of them are listed in *Ulrich's International Periodicals Directory*, a reference book that's almost certainly available at your public library. It is also available on CD-ROM and on the Web (for subscribers). You'll find many under the heading of "motion pictures," while others are listed under "communications—radio and television." Some deal with the creative and historical aspects of film, but the periodicals listed below are especially useful for persons interested in production jobs.

In addition, many more periodicals are published by organizations and companies with special interests in film and video. They are listed in *Audio Video Market Place*, a multimedia annual guide published by Information Today, Incorporated.

Although many of the annuals may be too expensive for an individual to purchase, you may be able to find them at your public library or request that a particular title or two be purchased. In addition, you can often buy sample copies of individual magazines by writing the publisher, enclosing a check, and asking for subscription information. That way, you can decide if a particular publication suits your needs. Purchase prices are listed in *Ulrich's International Periodicals Directory* and in other reference books.

If you're primarily interested in the technology of film and video production, check *Applied Science and Technology Index*, a database that exists on the Web and in print and is almost certain to be available at your public library. Frequent updates will give you a list of articles in various technical magazines. Publishers' addresses are listed in the index. Write and ask to buy the back issue with the article you're looking for and enclose the price of a sample copy of the magazine. This would be a good way to learn about different technical developments, including what's happening in high-definition television research.

If your interest is in the business aspect of film and video, you can keep up with developments by checking *Business Periodicals Index*, a similar index. Articles indexed here generally deal with management issues, stock ownership, and industry trends.

Benefits of Subscribing

Why should you keep up with periodicals or spend the money to purchase them? There are many facets to the film production industry. Unless you're studying film in Los Angeles, New York, or Chicago, chances are you won't keep current on changes and what they may mean to your job chances. Although $30 to $50 a year (a typical subscription price falls in this range) may seem expensive, and spending more than $150 for a twelve-month print subscription to *The Hollywood Reporter* or *Variety* may seem downright extravagant, a year's worth of reading such periodicals will give you an awareness of industry changes, names of "players," and a feeling for industry developments from an insider's point of view.

Many of these publications also have websites where you can read their headlines and some of the articles. Some may even allow you to sign up for an e-newsletter.

Below are suggested periodicals. They're published monthly, unless otherwise noted.

American Cinematographer
American Society of Cinematographers
Box 2230
Hollywood, CA 90078
theasc.com/magazine

Animation Magazine
30941 W. Agoura Rd., Ste. 102
Westlake Village, CA 91361
animationmagazine.net

Back Stage
(weekly)
Back Stage East
770 Broadway, 4th Fl.
New York, NY 10003
backstage.com

Boxoffice Magazine
155 S. El Molino Ave., Ste. 100
Pasadena, CA 91101
boxoff.com

Broadcast Engineering
9800 Metcalf
Overland Park, KS 66212-2215
broadcastengineering.com

DV Magazine
P.O. Box 1212
Skokie, IL 60076
dv.com/magazine

The Hollywood Reporter
(daily except Saturday, Sunday, holidays)
5055 Wilshire Blvd.
Los Angeles, CA 90036-4396
hollywoodreporter.com

Independent Film and Video Monthly
Association of Independent Video and Filmmakers (AIVF)
304 Hudson St., 6th Fl.
New York, NY 10013
aivf.org/independent

International Documentary Magazine
International Documentary Association
1201 W. Fifth St., Ste. M320
Los Angeles, CA 90017-1461
documentary.org/resources/magazine.html

Millimeter
Penton Publishing
122 E. 42nd St., Rm. 900
New York, NY 10168-0002
millimeter.com

MovieMaker Magazine
2265 Westwood Blvd., #479
Los Angeles, CA 90064
moviemaker.com

Premiere
Hachette Filipacchi Media U.S., Inc.
1633 Broadway
New York, NY 10019
premiere.com

Screen International
33-39 Bowling Green La.
London EC1 0DA
United Kingdom
screendaily.com

Television Week
(weekly)
6500 Wilshire Blvd., Ste. 2300
Los Angeles, CA 90048
tvweek.com

Variety
(weekly/daily)
5700 Wilshire Blvd., Ste. 120
Los Angeles, CA 90036
variety.com

Video Systems
Primedia Business Magazines and Media
9800 Metcalf Ave.
Overland Park, KS 66212-2215
videosystems.primediabusiness.com

Videography
United Entertainment Media, Inc.
460 Park Ave. South
New York, NY 10016
videography.com

Videomaker Magazine
(bimonthly)
York Publishing
Box 4591
Chico, CA 95927
videomaker.com

Wide Angle
(quarterly; emphasizes scholarship in film studies, criticism,
    international cinema, film history)
Johns Hopkins University Press
2715 N. Charles St.
Baltimore, MD 21218
muse.jhu.edu/journals/wide_angle

Appendix B

Film Commissions

Alaska Film Office
550 W. Seventh Ave., Ste. 1770
Anchorage, AK 99501-3510
907-269-8110
907-269-8125 (fax)
alaskafilm@dced.state.ak.us
dced.ak.us/trade/film

Arizona Film Commission
1700 W. Washington, Ste. 220
Phoenix, AZ 85007
800-523-6695
602-771-1193
602-280-1211 (fax)
commerce.state.az.us/film

Aspen Film Office
970-925-1031 (Aspen)
310-570-0575 (Los Angeles)
aps@aspenfilm.com
aspenfilm.com

Australian Film Commission
Level 4, 150 William St.
Woolloomooloo NSW 2011
G.P.O. Box 3984
Sydney NSW 2001
Australia
61-2-9321-6444
61-2-9357-3737 (fax)
info@afc.gov.au
afc.gov.au

British Columbia Film
2225 W. Broadway
Vancouver, BC V6K 2E4
Canada
604-736-7997
604-736-7290 (fax)
bcf@bcfilm.bc.aca
bcfilm.bc.ca

Chicago Film Office
1 N. LaSalle St.
Third Fl., Ste. 2165
Chicago, IL 60602
312-744-6415
312-744-1378 (fax)
chi.il.us/filmoffice

Colorado Springs Film Commission
515 S. Cascade Ave.
Colorado Springs, CO 80903
800-888-4748, ext. 131
719-635-7506, ext. 131
719-635-4968 (fax)
film@filmcoloradosprings.com
filmcoloradosprings.com

County Wicklow Film Commission
County Buildings
Wicklow Town, Ireland
353-404-20176
353-404-62136 (fax)

El Dorado Tahoe Film Commission
542 Main St.
Placerville, CA 95667
800-457-6279
530-626-4400
530-642-1624 (fax)
film@eldoradocounty.org
filmtahoe.com

Entertainment Industry Development Corporation (EIDC)/
    Los Angeles Film Office
7083 Hollywood Blvd., 5th Fl.
Hollywood, CA 90028
323-957-1000
323-463-0613 (fax)
info@eidc.com
eidc.com

Florida Film Commission
Governor's Office of Film and Entertainment
Executive Office of the Governor
The Capitol
Tallahassee, FL 32399-0001
877-FLA-FILM
850-410-4765
850-410-4770
filminflorida.com

Georgia Film, Video, and Music Office
285 Peachtree Center Ave. NE
Atlanta, GA 30303
404-656-3591
404-656-3565 (fax)
filmgeorgia.org

Inland Empire Film Commission
301 E. Vanderbilt Way, Ste. 100
San Bernardino, CA 92408
909-890-1090
909-890-1088 (fax)
filminlandempire.com

Irish Film Board
Rockfort House
St. Augustine St.
Galway, Ireland
353-91-561398
353-91-561405 (fax)
info@filmboard.ie
filmboard.ie

Maine Film Office
59 State House Station
111 Sewall St., 3rd Fl.
Augusta, ME 04333
207-624-7631
207-287-8070 (fax)
filmme@earthlink.net
filminmaine.com

Mississippi Film Office
Woolfolk State Office Bldg.
501 North West St., 5th Fl.
Jackson, MS 39201
601-359-3297
601-359-2112 (hotline)
601-359-5048 (fax)
visitmississippi.org/film

Montana Film Office
301 S. Park Ave.
Helena, MT 59620
800-553-4563
406-841-2876
406-841-2877 (fax)
montanafilm@visitmt.com
montanafilm.com

Montreal Film and TV Commission
303 Notre-Dame St. East, Level 2
Montreal, QC H2Y 3Y8
Canada
514-872-2883
514-872-3409 (fax)
film_tv@ville.montreal.qc.ca
montrealfilm.com

Nebraska Film Office
P.O. Box 98907
Lincoln, NE 68509-8907
800-228-4307
402-471-3680
info@filmnebraska.org
filmnebraska.org

Nevada Film Office
248 Mills St.
Grass Valley, NV 95945
nevadafilm.com
Las Vegas: 877-638-3456
lvnfo@bizopp.state.nv.us
Reno/Tahoe: 800-336-1600
ccnfo@bizopp.state.nv.us

New Mexico Film Commission
P.O. Box 20003
Santa Fe, NM 87504-5003
800-545-9871
505-827-9810
505-827-9799 (fax)
film@nmfilm.com
nmfilm.com

New York City Mayor's Office of Film, Theatre, and Broadcasting
1697 Broadway, #602
New York, NY 10019
212-489-6710
212-307-6237 (fax)
nyc.gov/html/filmcom

Northeast North Carolina Regional Film Commission
P.O. Box 29
Edenton, NC 27932
888-872-8562
252-482-4333
vrogers@ix.netcom.com
ncnortheast.com

Pacific Film and Television Commission
Level 15, 111 George St.
Brisbane, Queensland
Australia 4000
(+617) 32244144
(+617) 32246717 (fax)
pftc.com.au

Rhode Island Film and TV Office
RI Economic Development Corp.
1 W. Exchange St.
Providence, RI 02903
401-222-2601
401-273-8270 (fax)
rsmith@riedc.com
rifilm.com

Tennessee Film, Entertainment, and Music Commission
312 Eighth Ave. North
Tennessee Tower, 9th Fl.
Nashville, TN 37243-0405
877-818-345
615-532-2770
tn.film@state.tn.us
state.tn.us/film

Texas Film Commission
P.O. Box 13246
Austin, TX 78711
512-463-9200
512-463-4114
film@governor.state.tx.us
governor.state.tx.us/film

Toronto Film and Television Office
West City Hall, 2nd Fl.
Toronto, ON M5H 2N2
Canada
416-293-7570
416-392-0675
info@torontofilmpermits.com
torontofilmpermits.com

United Kingdom Film Council International
10 Little Portland St.
London W1W 7JG
United Kingdom
+44 (0) 20-7861-7860
+44 (0) 20-7861-7864 (fax)
internationalinfo@ukfilmcouncil.org.ujk
britfilmcom.co.uk

Utah Film Commission
324 S. State St., Ste. 500
Salt Lake City, UT 84111
800-453-8824
801-538-8740
801-538-8746 (fax)
film.utah.gov

Washington State Film and Video Office
2001 Sixth Ave., Ste. 2600
Seattle, WA 98121
206-256-6151
206-256-6154 (fax)
wafilm@cted.wa.gov
oted.wa.gov/ed/filmoffice

Western North Carolina Regional Film Commission
3 General Aviation Dr.
Fletcher, NC 28732
828-687-7234
828-687-7552
film @awnc.org
wncfilm.net

Wyoming Film Office
c/o Wyoming Travel Commission
214 W. Fifteenth St.
Cheyenne, WY 82002-0240
800-458-6657
307-777-3400
info@wyomingfilm.org
wyomingfilm.org

APPENDIX C

Film Schools

Academy of Art College
79 New Montgomery St.
San Francisco, CA 94105
800-544-ARTS
academyart.edu

APA International Film School
P.O. Box 362
Avalon, NSW 2107
Australia
(02) 9974 4480
apa.edu.au

Art Center College of Design
1700 Lida St.
Pasadena, CA 91103
626-396-2200
artcenter.edu

Bard College
Film and Electronic Arts Program
P.O. Box 5000
Annandale-on-Hudson, NY 12504
845-758-6822
bard.edu

Beijing Film Academy
International School
4# Xi Tu Cheng Rd.
Haidian District
Beijing 100088
P.R. China
86-10-8204-3748
bfa.edu.cn/bfa_english

Biola University
Mass Communication Program
13800 Biola Ave.
La Mirada, CA 90639
800-653-4652
biola.edu

Boston University
Department of Film and Television
College of Communication
640 Commonwealth Ave.
Boston, MA 02215
617-353-3450
bu.edu/com/filmtv

Brigham Young University
Department of Theatre and Media Arts
D-581 HFAC
Provo, UT 84602
801-422-6645
http://cfac.byu.edu/tma

Brooklyn College
Department of Film
2900 Bedford Ave.
0314 Plaza Bldg.
Brooklyn, NY 11210-2889
718-951-5664
http://depthome.brooklyn.cuny.edu/film

Brooks Institute of Photography
801 Alston Rd.
Santa Barbara, CA 93108
brooks.edu

Burlington College
Cinema Studies and Film Production
95 North Ave.
Burlington, VT 05401
800-862-9616
burlcol.edu

California Institute of the Arts (CalArts)
24700 McBean Parkway
Valencia, CA 91355
661-255-1050
calarts.edu

California State University, Fullerton
Department of Radio, TV, and Film
800 N. State College Blvd.
Fullerton, CA 92831
714-278-7883
fullerton.edu

California State University, Los Angeles
Department of Communication Studies
5151 State University Dr.
Los Angeles, CA 90032-8111
323-343-4200
calstatela.edu

California State University, Sacramento
Film Studies
Shasta Hall 104
Sacramento, CA 95819
916-278-6368
csus.edu

Cape Town International Film School
P.O. Box 17
Edgemead, 7407
South Africa
27 21 510 4013
film-school.tv

Carleton University
School for Studies in Art and Culture
423B St. Patrick's Bldg.
1125 Colonel By Dr.
Ottawa, ON K1S 5B6
Canada
613-520-5606
carleton.ca/artandculture

Chapman University
School of Film and Television
Cecil B. DeMille Hall
1 University Dr.
Orange, CA 92866
714-997-2400
chapman.edu

College for Creative Studies
Animation and Digital Media Department
201 E. Kirby
Detroit, MI 48202
800-952-ARTS
ccscad.edu

Columbia College, Chicago
600 S. Michigan Ave.
Chicago, IL 60605
312-663-1600
colum.edu

Columbia University
School of the Arts: Film
513 Dodge Hall
2960 Broadway
New York, NY 10027
212-854-2875
columbia.edu

Drexel University
College of Media Arts and Design
3141 Chestnut St.
Philadelphia, PA 19104
215-895-2386
http://drexel.edu/academics/comad/filmvideo/index.html

Eastern Michigan University
Department of Communication and Theatre Arts
124 Quirk Bldg.
Ypsilanti, MI 48197
313-487-3131
emich.edu/public/cta/tcom.html

Eastern Washington University
Electronic Media and Film
104 RTV
Cheney, WA 99004
509-359-6390
ewu.edu/cal/r_tv/programs.html

Emerson College
Department of Visual and Media Arts
120 Boylston St.
Boston, MA 02116
617-824-8500
emerson.edu

Florida State University Film School
University Center 3100A
Tallahassee, FL 32306
850-644-7728
http://filmschool.fsu.edu

Georgia State University
Department of Communication
1 Park Pl., 1040
Atlanta, GA 30302
404-651-4971
http://communication.gsu.edu

Humboldt State University
Department of Theatre, Film, and Dance
1 Harpst St.
Arcata, CA 95521
707-826-3011
humboldt.edu/~theatre/index.shtml

Hunter College
Department of Film and Media Studies
695 Park Ave.
Rm. 433 Hunter North
New York, NY 10021
212-772-4000
http://filmmedia.hunter.cuny.edu

Indiana University
Department of Communication and Culture
Mottier Hall (Ashton Center)
1790 E. Tenth St.
Bloomington, IN 47405
812-855-7217
indiana.edu/%7ecmcl/filmstud/filmindex.html

Ithaca College
Cinema and Photography Department
350 Park Hall, Ithaca College
Ithaca, NY 14850-7251
607-274-3011
ithaca.edu/rhp/cinephoto

Keene State College
229 Main St.
Keene, NH 03435
800-KSC-1909
keene.edu/programs/film

Los Angeles Film School
6363 Sunset Blvd., #400
Hollywood, CA 90028
877-9LA-FILM
lafilm.com

Loyola Marymount University
School of Film and Television
One LMU Dr., MC 8230
Los Angeles, CA 90045-8347
310-338-2737
lmu.edu/pages/590.asp

Manhattan School of Cinema
206 Bowery, 2nd Fl.
New York, NY 10012
212-941-7711
manhattanfilmschool.com

Miami International University of Art and Design (formerly known
    as International Fine Arts College)
1501 Biscayne Blvd., Ste. 100
Miami, FL 33132
800-225-9023
ifac.edu

Michigan State University
College of Communication Arts and Sciences
287 Communication Arts Bldg.
East Lansing, MI 48824
517-355-3410
cas.msu.edu

Montana State University
Department of Media and Theatre Arts
College of Arts and Architecture
P.O. Box 173350
Bozeman, MT 59717
406-994-3902
montana.edu

New York Film Academy
100 E. Seventeenth St.
New York, NY 10003
212-674-4300
nyfa.com

New York University
Tisch School of the Arts
22 Washington Sq. North
New York, NY 10011
212-998-4500
nyu.edu/tisch

North Carolina School of the Arts
School of Filmmaking
1533 S. Main St.
P.O. Box 12189
Winston-Salem, NC 27117
336-770-1471
ncarts.edu

Northern Michigan University
Communication and Performance Studies Dept.
203 Russell Thomas Fine Arts Bldg.
1401 Presque Isle Ave.
Marquette, MI 49855
906-227-2045
nmu.edu/caps

Northwestern University
Department of Radio/Television/Film
Frances Searle Bldg.
2240 Campus Dr.
Evanston, IL 60208
847-491-7530
communication.northwestern.edu

Ohio University
Honors Tutorial College Program in Film
35 Park Pl.
Athens, OH 45701
740-593-2723
ouhtc.org/film.php

Pennsylvania State University
Department of Film/Video and Media Studies
College of Communications
204 Carnegie Bldg.
University Park, PA 16802
814-865-2171
psu.edu/dept/comm/cstudent/film.html

Pratt Institute
School of Art and Design
Media Arts Program
200 Willoughby Ave.
Brooklyn, NY 11205
718-636-3633
pratt.edu

Purdue University
1080 Schleman Hall
West Lafayette, IN 47907
765-494-1776
purdue.edu

Rochester Institute of Technology
1 Lomb Memorial Dr.
Rochester, NY 14623-5603
585-475-2411
rit.edu

San Francisco Art Institute
800 Chestnut St.
San Francisco, CA 94133
sfai.edu/main.htm

San Francisco State University
Cinema Dept.
1600 Holloway Ave.
San Francisco, CA 94132
cinema.sfsu.edu

Savannah College of Art and Design
P.O. Box 3146
Savannah, GA 31402
800-869-7223
scad.edu

School of Visual Arts
Film and Video Department
209 E. Twenty-Third St.
New York, NY 10010-3994
schoolofvisualarts.edu

State University of New York
State University Plaza
Albany, NY 12246
518-443-5555
suny.edu

Syracuse University
Office of Admissions
201 Tolley Administration Bldg.
Syracuse, NY 13244-1100
315-443-3611
syr.edu

Temple University
1801 N. Broadway St.
Philadelphia, PA 19122
temple.edu/fma

University of Alabama
Box 870132
Tuscaloosa, AL 35487
800-933-BAMA (2262)
ua.edu

University of California, Los Angeles
UCLA School of Theater, Film, and Television
Department of Film, Television, and Digital Media
102 E. Melnitz Hall
Box 951622
Los Angeles, CA 90095-1622
filmtv.ucla.edu/filmtv

University of Canterbury
Department of Theatre and Film Studies
Private Bag 4800
Christchurch 8020
New Zealand
64 3 366 7001
drama.canterbury.ac.nz

University of Colorado
Regent Administrative Center 125
552 UCB
Boulder, CO 80309
303-492-6301
colorado.edu

University of Florida
Criser Hall
P.O. Box 114000
Gainesville, FL 32611
352-392-1374
ufl.edu

University of Iowa
Department of Cinema and Comparative Literature
425A English-Philosophy Bldg.
Iowa City, IA 52242-1527
uiowa.edu

University of Memphis
101 Wilder Tower
Memphis, TN 38152
901-678-2000
memphis.edu

University of Miami
School of Communication
Frances L. Wolfson Bldg.
P.O. Box 248127
Coral Gables, FL 33124-2104
miami.edu/com

University of Michigan
Program in Film and Video Studies
2512 Frieze Bldg.
105 S. State St.
Ann Arbor, MI 48109
lsa.umich.edu/filmvideo

University of New Orleans
Lakefront
2000 Lakeshore Dr.
New Orleans, LA 70148
800-256-5866
uno.edu

University of Southern California
School of Cinema-Television
209 Lucas Bldg.
University Park Campus, CA 90089-2211
usc.edu/school/cntv

University of Texas at Austin
Department of Radio-Television-Film
1 University Station A0800
Austin, TX 78712-0108
utexas.edu/coc/rtf

University of Utah
Division of Film Studies
375 South, 1530 East
Rm. 257B
Salt Lake City, UT 84112
801-581-5127
film.utah.edu

University of Wisconsin, Madison
Communication Arts
6117 Vilas Hall
821 University Ave.
Madison, WI 53706
commarts.wisc.edu

Watkins College of Art and Design
2298 MetroCenter Blvd.
Nashville, TN 37228
615-383-4848
watkins.edu/programs/film/index.html

York University
150 Atkinson Bldg.
4700 Keele St.
Toronto, ON M3J 1P3
Canada
416-736-5000
yorku.ca/finearts

About the Authors

As a child in a Pennsylvania coal-mining town, Jan Bone remembers eagerly saving and spending her modest allowance for admission to the movies. Every Saturday she'd stand in line, waiting to see the cowboy stars gallop across the big screen. Each all-too-brief episode ended with a cliff-hanger requiring fans to come back the following Saturday to learn the outcome.

Jan's fascination with film apparently was passed on to one of her sons. When Chris Bone was eleven, he and a group of friends taught themselves animation, creating cartoons about imaginary space aliens and renting a Super-8 camera. By the time Chris was a high school senior, his films had won national Kodak and Chicago student film festival awards. Chris graduated from the University of Southern California as a cinema major, and his job search and subsequent career in the film industry made Jan realize the need for this book.

Jan, a graduate of Cornell University with an M.B.A. in marketing from Roosevelt University, is a prolific freelance writer. She is senior writer of the *Chicago Tribune*'s special advertising sections;

lead writer for Rand McNally's *Bank Notes*, a newsletter for financial institutions; and a writer for National Safety Council publications. Her work has appeared in magazines as diverse as *Family Circle*, *Woman's World*, and *Food Engineering*. Jan has also coauthored (with Ron Johnson) *Understanding the Film: An Introduction to Film Appreciation*.

Jan has been listed in *Who's Who of American Women*. She has won local, state, and national writing awards. She is an associate member of the Society of Manufacturing Engineers.

She is married, the mother of four married sons, and the grandmother of Emily Diane.

Ana Fernandez is a graduate of the University of Michigan, where she concentrated in film/video studies and psychology. She lives in New York City, where she has worked on a number of different television series and theater productions.